I dedicate this book to the person who put a spurious advertisement in *Exchange and Mart* on May 27 1982 when I was in hospital undergoing spinal traction. The advertisement stated 'Plummer's Merle for sale £65 genuine reason for sale.' Perhaps the contents of this book will show how ridiculous that advertisement was.

I should also like to dedicate this book to Ron Davis, a fellow teacher who during my most serious illness helped me out of a very tight spot – and shut up about it!

MERLE

The Start of a Dynasty

D. BRIAN PLUMMER

PHOTOGRAPHY BY
DAVID HANCOCK

TIDELINE

British Library Cataloguing-in-Publication Data
A catalogue record for this book is available from
the British Library

ISBN   978-1-906486-25-9

First Published 1982

Tideline Publications Promotions

49 Kinmel Street
Rhyl
Denbighshire
LL18 1AG

Mixed Sources
Product group from well-managed
forests and other controlled sources
www.fsc.org Cert no. SGS-COC-1722
© 1996 Forest Stewardship Council

FSC

Printed in the UK by Butler and Tanner (ISO14001) on Forest Stewardship
Council certified paper using vegetable inks.

CONTENTS

MERLE: THE START OF A DYNASTY

Merle: Start of a Dynasty

I *Of Dai Fish and Lurchers Generally*

Ironically, I never met Dai Fish, and I say ironically, for without Dai I should not have started breeding that particular dynasty, without Dai I should not have had Merle, and without Merle, I should never have begun this book.

Lurchers were not my first love. Far from it. The village in which I grew up was a mining slum in the South Welsh coalfield, an area of slag piles, rubbish dumps watered by a filthy coal-filled brook. It was hardly the place to find use for a lurcher for you needed to walk ten miles to see a rabbit. Hence my interest in lurchers was nurtured by what I now consider to be the semi-fictitious writings of Taplin and Brian Vesey-FitzGerald, who talked of incredibly sagacious animals lurking romantically beneath Romany waggons or *vardos*, of sly racy dogs, insidious as a whisper, poaching estates by themselves and returning home with their stolen swag, of dogs stealthily avoiding gamekeepers, knowing instinctively who was a foe and who was as disreputable as their roguish masters.

I read avidly and absorbed tales of canny dogs whose intelligence far exceeded that of an Alsatian or even that of their itinerant owners. Of dogs which, when their owners were nabbed by gamekeepers, would act as if they were nothing to do with them. At night I would sit enraptured by tales of poachers like the Arighos, gipsies or 'tinklers' they are called in the borders, who, according to FitzGerald, trained dogs to an incredible pitch of efficiency, so that they became instruments of poaching, dexterous thieving extensions of their owners' hands. These were men who, according to FitzGerald, carefully kept true breeding strains of lurcher, incredibly bright and tractable dogs, trained as only gipsies knew how. It was great stuff to stimulate the adolescent mind of a boy who was, at the age of ten, already contemplating leaving home at the earliest possible moment. It was immensely interesting to a lad already sufficiently interested in hunting to forget the humdrum world of the academic, to a boy who found Dickens impossibly hard but *The Dog Crusoe* fascinating. As it transpired, however, the Romany tales were hopelessly romantic nonsense.

By the time I was old enough to own a lurcher of my own, the breed, or type would be more accurate to say, had probably undergone a transformation. The boom period after the Second World War, a time when men made overnight fortunes by buying piles of antiquated tanks and selling them as scrap metal (literally swords hammered into plough shares) had altered the way of life of the itinerant. The peg-selling Romany of my youth, still living in horse-drawn *vardos* or bender tents made from ash saplings covered in canvas little changed since the time of Borrow, had given way to flash, cowboy-hatted extroverts, grown rich and slothful on the proceeds of selling scrap and laying cut-price tarmac. The hop-picking, potato-gathering bands, specializing in duckering and poaching, had now become dwellers in expensive chrome-plated caravans, pulled along by almost new and invariably untaxed Mercedes and Volvos. If the gipsy had changed his way of life, so had his dogs changed.

Foraging, self-poaching, useful dogs, dogs capable of keeping a family in meat ranging from pheasant to hedgehog, were no longer prized. True, there are still lurchers of a type kept and even bred by travellers, but they were not of the type described by Taplin or FitzGerald. Now a new sort of dog was required by the travellers, a type that could be bundled into the back of a wagon, transported to some spot a few miles distant and turned loose on a hare while their owners wagered on the outcome of the course. A sagacious dog was not required, a hunter using his nose and brain to come upon its prey was no longer deemed useful. In fact, many lurcher-owning travellers at the annual Appleby fair told me they'd give away a dog that had 'nose'. What was wanted was a near greyhoundy type of beast, small of brain but strong of muscle; and silent, of course, for few itinerants have permission on the land they course. So, new breeds of dogs, dogs totally alien to the old-fashioned Romany life, were added to the gipsy lurchers to increase their speed. Deerhound, greyhound and, horror of horror, saluki blood now entered into the lineage of lurchers, and, with this increased speed, with this increased height and power, came a brainlessness, a stupidity, an intractability that was alien to the genuine lurcher of old. These dogs, the result of massive infusions of sight-hound blood, could often take hare well enough, there was no denying, but few would have the sense to check at a placed long net or drive a hare into the meshes of a gate net. Fewer still had the instinct to hunt alone, catch their prey and hightail it for home, avoiding gamekeeper and country bobby, landowner and layabout, to deposit their prey at their owner's door. Indeed, even the legendary lurcher loyalty, the sort that gave undying fidelity to the poaching owner, was

2

Deerhound

lost by this injudicious addition of sight-hound blood. The new
lurcher could be swopped, sold, traded without harm to its brainless
personality, and, seconds after arriving at its new home, would settle
in as if it had been born in the place. A lurcher was no longer the dog
of the sly poacher, the village disreputable, the night-time skulker
with sewn-in pockets to carry stolen game. Now any dog who could
be taken on a piece of string, slipped and coursed at a hare was called
a lurcher, and by the time I became old enough to own and keep a
lurcher, the type of dog I required was as much an anachronism as a
dinosaur.

Well, at sixteen years of age I did leave home, and it was to be some
years before I could keep dogs on premises I could reasonably call my
own. The state of the true lurcher had declined even further by this
time. During the late 1950s, some country shows staged classes for
lurchers. At first there were few entries, as the lurcher still carried the

hallmark of the disreputable and the dogs entered wouldn't have won many prizes at a beauty competition. There were still some who bred an old Norfolk type of dog at that time, sagacious dogs free from the taint of deerhound, saluki and excessive greyhound blood, but the shows and the obsession for conformation soon altered that. Bigger dogs, faster, more racy dogs, were now appearing, a far cry from the lurchers of Taplin and an even further cry from the dogs described in *It's My Delight*. And with this concern for conformation came a lack of interest in canine intelligence or, above all, tractability, and at this somewhat sorry point in time my interest in lurchers began.

My first lurchers were sleek, rough-coated dogs of greyhoundy shape and reputedly of greyhound to collie to greyhound breeding. I say reputedly, for in spite of the fact I have bred the genuine article, I have never produced a rough coat from dogs of this breeding. These dogs were fast, agile and game, but it would be a joke to call them tractable, an exaggeration even to refer to them as biddable, and after a while it became obvious why. By dint of mating a half-brother to a half-sister, I succeeded in producing a dog that would have passed as a show-bred saluki, an elegant, dainty, fastidious hare-brained dog that, when given to a friend, proved its obvious oriental ancestry by coming a capricious, stupid animal, which, even as it became more than a passable hare courser, also became an even more dexterous chicken killer and sheep worrier – qualities which brought about not only its destruction but also its owner's financial ruin when the dog ran amuck through a batch of newly imported French rams brought into the country for an expensive eugenics project.

Advertisements are often deceptive, their sole purpose being to convince people that the article for sale is the one they seek. Hence, like Ponce de Leon, I followed up each and every advertisement for a genuine gipsy lurcher, hoping that each and every one might be the real McCoy, a tractable, biddable, natural hunter, a canine sneak thief, capable of wreaking havoc on any game estate, while I, from the comfort of my only chair, waited for it to return laden with booty, weighted down with pheasant and hares. But, also like Ponce de Leon, I returned empty-handed – educated a little perhaps convinced of human gullibility and deceit certainly, but empty-handed nevertheless. I must have explored every council estate in Britain, seen every form of canine (and human) cur, been told obviously ridiculous lies, offered monstrous travesties of dogs, and once had my car broken into while looking at a most unlikely litter. I heard stories of how such and such a dog was line bred from the dogs of such and such a band of travellers, how people lived from lamping these dogs, how certain dogs were responsible for the postponing of that year's Waterloo Cup.

4

I was told amazing tales which convinced me that either the teller was mad or the raconteur thought I was madder. Once, when I asked for a demonstration of how biddable a certain dog was, its owner, after much protest, levered open a coal-house door. A huge black beast leaped out, raced off and, in the best fairy-tale tradition, was never seen again.

Appleby Fair should have been the place to buy a genuine gipsy dog if there ever was one. It was certainly the place to meet genuine Romanies. It was there that I met Charlie Ingrams, a famous Romany and, like all genuine Romanies, a great raconteur and teller of Romany tales. Charlie was a famous weaver of dreams, the type of man who has captivated audiences around a thousand camp fires throughout history. I questioned him on genuine Romany dogs, using my knowledge of his language to open a door into a world now long gone, for Charlie was eighty then, and is long dead.

He laughed at my questions and shook his head. Yes, there were such dogs he explained, but FitzGerald had been fooled by the gipsy bands with whom he travelled. Such dogs were born and not the production of training. Their instincts and natural talents were exploited rather than taught. Furthermore, Charlie added, few books concerning Romanies and Romany ways are reliable, for a Romany will tell a researcher only that which the researcher wants to believe. Chicken thieves, called *Kannechors* among the Romanies, were dogs who developed this particular inbred quality, for it was impossible to *train* a dog to creep belly down to a flock of feeding fowl and snatch exactly the right one, retrieving it alive and unharmed to the owner. Then Charlie lapsed into a tale of a time between the wars, a time that saw the end of much gipsy family life, a time when the Rom forsook the *vardo* for the life of a *keremengro*, the world of the house dweller. Charlie's eyes took on a far-away look as he told the tale.

'I had a dog once – he paused to remember the date perhaps. 'That was useless at *shoshoi* [hares] and precious little on drummers [rabbits], but Christ, he could steal chickens, Christ, could he, chor. About that time,' he tapped out his pipe like a rustic Bulldog Drummond getting ready for a tale, 'I was cock fighting regular, like with most of the travellers in North Wales, tinkers, *didikais*, the lot. At that time the cock of the hoop was a *didikai* called Ryland, him who was descended from Old Ryland who was hanged for cut-pursing, so they say. Ryland kept a strain of black reds, not Derby type nor Oxford game, but better battlers there just weren't, and they'd kill in the shuffle afore another cock got started. Ryland beat everyone. Not just travellers, but gorgios, doctors, solicitors, schoolteachers' – he eyed me up and down, his eyes twinkling – 'anyone who fancied a chance at trying their hand at something a bit naughty or illegal – just like you do, Bri, I suppose,' he added mischievously.

'Well', he continued, 'Ryland's stuff steeled me greys to pieces. So I ups and tries to buy a cock from him to get the blood, but he just laughed at us and wouldn't even part with eggs lessen they were "shook"' – eggs that are shaken violently will not hatch. 'Well, I determined myself to get one of his'nt or be buggered and killed doing it. So I takes the dog to his pitch [caravan site] and Ryland shows off his cocks a treat, even going telling us how such and such a cock was bred, from which hens he came, and from which cock he was got, boasting like buggery, though I suppose he had cause enough to boast what with him being cock of the hoop from Wales to Scotland. "Feel dis bird," he would say, offering us a cock bird or a hen, for even Ryland's hens would fight just about owt, but I was careful to only handle one cock bird, a fine black red that had fought six mains, hard mains too, and was cut to buggery, but not through the breeds [genital organs]. Well, no way was he selling him, and who'd blame him, so I rode back to my own camp, watching Ryland go into his caravan still bragging to himself. Half a mile later I nods to the dog and he hares it back to Ryland's and gets back with the red cock in his mouth, the cock angry and squawking hell but not hurt too bad to fly, fight or breed. We put him on a farm near Egremont, and though Ryland was angry he couldn't prove a bloody thing. He was killed in a bombing raid in 1940, a raid in Bristol or Coventry, I think,' he added wistfully. 'Ryland, I mean,' he explained, 'not the cock.'

'What happened to the dog?' I put in, cutting off a reminiscence that wouldn't have interested me.

Charlie thought for a minute. 'I swapped him for a motor bike,' he answered after a minute's pause, smashing forever my faith in the value that travellers are supposed to place on their poaching dogs. Never would a gipsy sell one, Vesey-FitzGerald had written!

I related this incident to Henry Tegner, a naturalist *par excellence* and one hell of an authority on all things countrified. Henry laughed.

'Yes,' he confessed, 'I really enjoyed *It's My Delight*, but the notion that there ever were Romany strains of lurcher is a bit romantic, a little unlikely and such dogs belong in fiction alongside *Dumbell of Brookfield*, dogs credited with human rather than animal intelligence. Slightly far fetched,' he added, puncturing what was left of my dream of owning a genuine poaching, thieving, dishonest-to-goodness lurcher.

'Did you ever see a lurcher strain among the Romanies in the North?' I persisted.

'I never yet met a traveller of any sort that wasn't permanently

6

Saluki

buying and selling dogs,' he answered, and then, tiring of the conversation perhaps, he added, 'If you want this ideal dog, I think you'll have to breed one yourself, not try to buy a puppy from someone. Draw up a list of the qualities you want and those you don't want and breed your dog. Of course, it will take time,' he continued, 'but time, as you keep telling me, is the only thing of which you seem to have plenty.'

It was, of course, excellent advice. Start from scratch. Add only what you want to the strain, being careful not to add too much grey-hound, and ruthlessly cull anything that is inferior, breeding in a particular type a particular marking to characterize the strain and prevent wandering itinerants helping themselves to your stock. Thus I would forsake my elegant, deerhoundy strain, a strain that was winning shows galore for me, avoid like the plague any saluki blood, and settle for a tractable, biddable base line, lightly laced with greyhound for speed. By breeding only from those who displayed distinct poaching instincts, or an ability to steal and avoid detection, gradually – and gradually seemed to be the operative word – I would breed my strain. I would shut my ears to those who advised adding such and such a breed to produce a good coursing dog, for competitive coursing dogs were the very last things I wanted. The base line was to prove the first stumbling-block, however.

Two lines, two breeds of dog, suggested themselves. First, a retriever might prove a fair start, for retrievers are natural hunters with excellent noses. Their very name implies a natural aptitude to return game to hand or, better still, to home. Two sorts of retriever were available. First, labradors, which I considered too heavy, and secondly, the golden retriever, which, when mated to a greyhound, produced a broken-coated cur-like dog. I'd seen a man produce useful varminty dogs using this cross. However, on the debit side, retrievers are natural sycophants, anybody's dogs, second only to greyhounds in lack of loyalty, for they were bred to be hired out to visiting hunters, gun men who wanted a few days' shooting in the country without keeping a dog of their own in their town flat. Hence a dog was bred that changed hands easily, a dog that was docile and easily managed, totally unsuspicious of strangers, namely, the golden retriever. These were not the qualities I wanted in my lurcher strain, I was certain. A dog which caught quarry was all well and good, but a dog that retrieved it to all and sundry, friend and foe alike, was not what I required. A dog that was suspicious of strangers was to be the essence of my future lurcher strain, and in saying this I needed to look no further.

I was born in shepherding country and I live in cattle country, so the second choice of dog to use as a base line for my future lurcher strain had to be a collie. The reasons were obvious. No breed is more suspicious of strangers or more reserved. Few dogs have greater stamina, though stamina is not a quality I particularly value in a lurcher bred to provide for the pot rather than simply for coursing hares. And, as an added bonus, most collies have good noses – though for the life of me I can't see why, for herding doesn't require a good nose. The greatest bonus, however, is the legendary collie intelligence. There is no dog whose brain can compare with that of the collie, and I speak as someone who has trained most dogs. I've seen collies whip the backsides off spaniels in retrieving, and I watched one fetch a wounded mallard off the River Severn in flood conditions that would terrify a labrador. I've seen them catch rabbits, rob snares, kill foxes and even draw badgers. If one has the sense

8

Smithfield-type collie – a dog that actually herds droves and hunts

and patience to understand their natures, there is virtually nothing they can't do.

On the debit side, few first-cross dogs 'twixt collie and greyhound are capable of taking hare since most are a shade too heavy. The second crosses, greyhound to greyhound to collie, lose most of their canny nature and many resemble damn-nigh pure greyhounds in temperament as well as appearance. Mind you, when a first cross favours the greyhound in shape the result is unbeatable, but these are rarities, though I've seen them.

A last drawback is that the first crosses are a bit ugly, and I mean ugly. It is not a serious problem, and I'm scarcely a Beau Brummel myself, but they are sufficiently undistinctive to be worth standard-izing into a true breeding strain. Somewhere 'twixt a three-quarter-bred dog and a half-bred dog seemed to be the desired lurcher, a dog with great speed but one not lacking in brain either. I'd settled for a

9

border collie and was intending to breed something collie-blooded but distinctive when I had a phone call from Dai Fish.

As I said, I never actually met Dai Fish, but a friend of his once visited my menagerie of ferrets and dogs and I just happened to mention that I intended breeding my own collie strain of lurcher. Two days later, out of the blue, Dai Fish phoned and mentioned that he'd mate his collie bitch to a greyhound dog and let me have a puppy – free of charge. Dai seemed to be that sort of person. As it transpired, he was on his backside financially at the time, but a peculiar generosity seemed to be the hallmark of Dai. From the tales I've heard about him, money didn't concern him. When he had money he spent it, when he was broke, he bided his time until his ship (a small boat in Dai's case) came in.

When the puppies arrived, sired by a big track greyhound dog (no record breaker, unlike almost every flapping track dog I've ever encountered!), a merle puppy was one among the litter of seven. Dai didn't even have the money to rail the dog, but he still refused payment for the pup.

Two friends, Joe and Ernie, fetched the puppy, very prematurely weaned since the bitch had no milk and Dai wanted her working sheep again anyway. The dog was scarcely an impressive puppy, white-faced, blue merle and terrified, a mite of scarcely three weeks old. Even in his infancy – an appealing time in most dogs' lives – he was decidedly ugly by any standards. Joe and Ernie watched for my expression as, like two rather sheepish conjurers, they produced the puppy from behind Joe's back. My expression was probably predictable. Merle was scarcely what I'd hoped for to start a dynasty, but a gift horse is a gift horse and a look in the mouth is not only churlish but unreasonable. There that evening I phoned Dai to thank him for the gift, but though I let the phone ring for twenty minutes or so, there was no answer, and it was to be three days before I learnt why. That evening Dai had gone to work in the local drift mine and been burned to death in a pit accident. As I've said, I never got round to meeting Dai Fish.

2 Some Facts about Merle-Coloured Dogs

'Don't like 'em,' sniffed Mo, 'and wouldn't have one as a gift. Nor would any of "the people" either.'

Mo has been settled for twenty years, lived in a council house, worked as a keeper, but still calls the Romany 'the people', his people perhaps. He elaborated on his comment.

'Most have white eyes, which ain't natural in any beast, tame or wild, and they are considered unlucky – the tinks calls 'em moonpies, and most will avoid settling on farms where they are kept. Had a bad experience with one of the bastards meself.'

He sniffed, but then refused to go on with the tale. I knew what he meant, for I, too, had had a bad experience with one of 'them merle uns'.

I had been twelve at the time, and earning pocket money by delivering groceries around the hill farms that surrounded the mining valley in which I lived, hill farms reached only by straight up-and-down paths on forty-five-degree gradients. On the day in question, I had opened a gate across the lane leading up to a farm, when I experienced a violent blow between the shoulder blades and a stabbing pain in my sides. I crashed earthwards, spilling the groceries across the path (it's strange, but I can still remember the Brooke Bond save-the-stamps packet falling in the mud) and tried to roll to throw off my assailant, only to find I was gazing into the jaws of a large merle farm cur, not quite pure bred enough to be called collie, who fixed me with his apparently sightless wall eyes, his mouth dripping slaver into my upturned face. Today I teach in a rough area, and am constantly told by various scrawny fifteen-year-old machos how they could kill a fully grown police-trained Alsatian simply by pulling its front legs apart, thereby bursting its heart. Now, even if such Herculean feats were possible, and I assure the reader they are not, another overriding factor comes into play when a large predator (such as a dog) tackles its prey. As soon as the victim of a predatory attack receives a deep and agonizing wound, a chemical reaction is triggered off and a blood-carried pain-killing drug anaesthetizes the body. Hence the apparent indifference of wildebeeste as Cape hunting dogs mangle their vicera – the highlight of many of David Attenborough's television films (strange how people find disembowelled wildebeeste little short of fascinating). Now, it is all well and good to anaesthetize an organ when absolute agony would be the natural result of such an injury, but the cessation of pain is not without its dangers, for the injured beast usually gives up the ghost when so tranquillized and ceases to fight. This allows the predator to finish its task, a process that makes one think that God must be some hideous prankster with a PhD in organic chemistry. Yet it is a process that enables prey and predator to maintain the balance of life on this planet.

This philosophy did not actually occur to me as I lay bestraddled by the collie, though I was certainly conscious of my inability to summon any strength to fight off the dog. I can, to this day, remember those awful white eyes, more terrifying than the teeth it seemed at the time, gazing down into my face, eyes more fitting to a lunar beast than a border collie. How long I lay there I will never know, though it seemed an eternity, but eventually the dog left me lying, to attack someone else, I believe. Yes, I knew exactly what Moses meant, and I was mistrustful of merle-coloured collies from that day onwards.

Merle colouring has long been a suitable subject for myth and legend, and the legends have a sprinkling of truth woven into the fabric of nonsense. No two merles are alike, and the markings are as distinctive as human finger-prints. Some are heavily marked with black, some are suffused with tan, others are sooty and some even nearly black. Only a fool of a dog thief would steal a merle-coloured lurcher, Moses had said, and there was a basis for truth in this statement, for merle lurchers were extremely rare at the time when I acquired the Dai Fish puppy, though they are far more common now. Furthermore, not all merle-coloured animals are wall eyed, not by a long chalk. In fact, only one in every sixteen of the merles I have bred has been wall eyed. Dai Fish had said during one of our telephone conversations, 'No set of eyes on merle collies are ever exactly the same,' and while I had with scientific thoroughness, as I thought, questioned this statement, I now know it to be true. Some merles have normal eyes, having the same pigment as the eyes of other dogs, others are ticked with white pigment, or more accurately ticked with the absence of normal pigment. It is fairly rare to find a merle with both eyes ticked, but odd-eyed merles, merles with one eye of normal colour and the other eye 'wall', are very common. All in all, dog thieves who steal merle-coloured dogs are begging for trouble, and in

The hypnotic wall eye

the area where I live, plagued as it is by tinkers, such a distinctive type of dog would prove more than useful.

Next fallacy about to be exploded. Wall eyes are not in any way inferior in vision to ordinary eyes, and although there is usually a 'blind' expression on the faces of most wall-eyed animals, there is no evidence to suggest that the 'eye' is related to any form of blindness. A great number of collies do go blind, particularly those bred from certain trial-bred strains, but this peculiarity is due to the 'collie eye anomaly', a defect found in collies and related breeds. Now, merle-coloured trial dogs are rare, to say the least, so contrary to merle collies being more prone to blindness they may even show a lower incidence of blindness than ordinary coloured dogs. In fact, one folk explanation for the expression 'wall eye' is that when horses manifested this peculiarity, a person selling the horse tried to keep the pigmentless eye to the wall, so that the eye would pass unnoticed until after the business transaction was completed, for wall eyes in horses are considered to be blind or defective eyes.

Now, enter the dragon! Behind every legend is a grain or so of truth, and at this point it will be expedient to explain a little about the

A rare black merle puppy

A silver merle puppy

A red merle puppy

breeding of merles. Merle collie puppies are invariably produced by mating a merle collie to an ordinary black and white collie, the resulting litter being roughly fifty per cent merle and fifty per cent black and white. There are, in fact, no true breeding strains of merle, or merle and white collies, and for good reason. A merle dog mated to a merle bitch throws all manner of evils. Three quarters of the litter would admittedly be merle, and merles without obvious genetic defects, but the remaining quarter would be white, and some of these white puppies would have the real no-nonsense defects the breeders of old associated with whiteness. Not only are these white puppies usually constitutionally weak, but some have horrendous eye problems and, as an added inverted bonus, some are also deaf.

A lady from Cheltenham once wrote to me to tell me how she had deliberately mated two merle border collies together, against the advice of her vet, and how the litter produced caused her considerable heartache. Of the five puppies born, two were white and three were merle, one silver merle, one black merle. Both whites were blind. Indeed, it was obvious from a week or so old that one had no eye sockets. The other white puppy had pale wall eyes and no pupils to admit light to the retina. Both lived an unhappy three months of stumbling into furniture, kennels and litter mates before the woman finally hardened her heart and had the poor little devils put to sleep.

No, there are no true breeding strains of merle collies, and puppies accidentally produced from merle to merle mating have fairly certainly given rise to the legendary peculiarities associated with merle colouring. Yet the merles bred from these matings are very rarely defective.

Well, I mustn't spoil the tale with data about breeding and genetics, so back to the story and the puppy I received from Dai Fish. I'd estimated Merle's age at the time of arrival at four four and a half weeks, though he might have been a shade older, for four-week-old puppies are not able to focus all that well and most regard any hand as 'friendly'. Merle was able to focus all right, and he looked far from friendly as he crouched, petrified, stained by his own filth and vomit beneath my settee. If I approached, he urinated or vomited. If I tried to pick him up, he literally froze, becoming rigid as a rock, his eyes glazed with terror. At first I thought he could be one of those nervous dogs, neurotic wrecks which cringe away from friend and foe alike and wreak havoc on anyone who follows up the relationship. Shy biters, the dog books call them. For a moment, I confess the thought did cross my mind, but such dogs are not usually the product of injudicious breeding so much as the result of very bad handling. Neurotic people not genetics usually make neurotic dogs. Merle's condition was fairly obviously the result of being yanked away from his dam prematurely, being crated up in a box in total darkness and then whipped out like the props of an undexterous conjurer for inspection. Early weaning can have a decidedly deleterious effect on a dog, and that is an understatement.

Pups taken from their dams before time, however, are usually remarkably tractable, and for very good reasons, particularly if kept isolated from other dogs. Darwin, in *The Voyage of a Naturalist*, tells of shepherds in Patagonia who took rough-coated male Spanish shepherd dogs (dogs that were probably kin of Smithfield type collies, although most European herding breeds look alike) from their dams before time allowed them to suckle tied-down ewes for sustenance, and kept them totally isolated from other dogs. As soon as the dogs' testicles descended, they were castrated to stifle any sexual urges that might attract them to other dogs and were fed only by the shepherd. Obviously, this sort of treatment tended to warp the dog's personality (I certainly wouldn't like it happening to me, for sure), but dogs so treated didn't regard themselves as canine, but considered themselves ovine and attacked any animal or human that caused harm to or threatened the safety of the flock. It is also curious that the flock, when threatened, ran immediately to the sanctuary offered by the dog, who stood there like a lead ram guarding them from predators.

Funnily enough, as I write this I glance down at Balaam and Barak who are two of Merle's beautiful elegant streamlined sons, the progeny of Merle and a top-grade coursing greyhound bitch, and my mind flashes back to that first day in my relationship with Merle. I can still picture him crouching under that settee, petrified with fear, thrust into a totally alien and baffling world, but at the time I admit that all I could think of was what a hideous-looking dog he appeared to be.

Forcing oneself on a puppy of this type is not the thing to do, though some puppies love it. The result of such treatment can be devastating, for the babe tends to 'withdraw' into itself still further, making any form of social contact with the dog almost impossible. In fact, I've seen nervous puppies slip into a state of near catatonia when their owners have persisted in trying to make contact with them. A puppy of this ilk, like Lorenz's primitive cats, must come to the trainer, not vice versa, if any relationship is to be established. So I resolved to sit it out in the same room as the puppy until he decided to make the first overtures, and I was fairly confident I should not have long to wait. Collies and collie hybrids are the most intelligent of dogs, and curiosity is the hallmark of all intelligent mammals. I was confident that, within an hour or so of his arrival, he would decide to

Balaam and Barak, two of Merle's sons

investigate me, come out of his state of terror and all would be well. At ten o'clock that night I resolved that by eleven I would have the puppy frantic to please me. I could not have been more wrong.

Joe, Ernie and Joe's son stayed the night, so I spent it in a chair, reading, dozing and watching the puppy. T. H. White says in *The Goshawk* that, as soon as an animal has confidence enough to sleep in the presence of a person, one is half-way through the training. He could be correct, for this method certainly works well with hawks. If I kept perfectly still, the merle puppy under the chair stayed relaxed, but if I stood to leave, he froze to a rigid terrified statue. If I approached the settee he simply voided a flood of urine and diarrhoea and curled into an almost foetal position. For one awful moment I had doubts as to whether I could do anything with the beast, or even whether this colour was somehow connected to intractability. The notion was unscientific, however, when viewed in the light of all that

18

the puppy had endured during his short life, but there was little change in him during the next day or so, except for a gradual lessening of his awful diarrhoea. What was bad was that he refused food, and worse still he refused a drink. Now it is good, indeed standard practice to starve a puppy or adult with bad diarrhoea, for dehydration follows rapidly if a puppy is allowed to feed while it has an intestinal disorder. My diary for this time, still unpleasantly scented with the stench of dog excreta that pervaded my house during Merle's early days, reads, 'I am fairly certain he will die for it is unlikely any small young animal can survive such debilitating diarrhoea. If I get him to a vet it will be a further setback, and if he has to have an antibiotic injection it may prevent any link with him being formed.' The next three days passed and I continued to sleep in the chair of my foetid living room, waiting for the death of the puppy or a lightning raid by the public health to bring the experiment to an end. However, on the fourth day I awoke with a start around 3.30 a.m. to find my hand being nudged by the puppy. From then on we never looked back.

He fed that day, tiny amounts of cooked flesh liberally dusted with bone flour as an astringent to stop the ghastly flux of the bowels. More important still, he drank. It is, however, bad stockmanship to allow a sick and ailing puppy to drink copious amounts of water at one sitting as a distended stomach tends to induce vomiting, and heyho, we're back to square one with dehydration going lickety-spit as the puppy loses water from both anus and mouth. He was nervous, though, and while he followed me around when I carried his water dish, at the first sign of Ernie or Joe he vanished under the settee again and the air became filled with a foul stench as he evacuated his bowels in terror. Yet, by nightfall, he was nosing a golf ball I had picked up during a poaching escapade on our local golf course, mouthing it, dropping it and following it around the room. I was fairly certain he would be an enthusiastic retriever.

Retrieving is a peculiar instinct, for it involves a twofold process consisting of two activities seemingly in conflict. First, the dog must want the object it is to retrieve badly enough to chase after it and pick it up. Then, by complete contrast, he must be prepared to bring that desired object back to his human owner. Sight hounds, that is grey-hounds, deerhounds and worst of all salukis, are notoriously bad retrievers, and most will simply stand over a fallen object, be it a dummy or a slain quarry, and guard it aimlessly for a few minutes before either leaving it or worse still eating it. Thus, any dog with sight-hound blood must be well and truly schooled in retrieving as a babe or all is lost. I would take my hat off to any trainer who could

A black merle

take up a four-year-old saluki and turn it into a competent retriever (or competent anything, for that matter). Hence, retrieving is best taught when the dog is a babe, a puppy with a puppy's sense of fun, for retrieving has to be fun to be successful.

Sight hounds, or lurchers with a great deal of sight-hound blood, tend to become serious, or maybe lose their sense of fun, fairly early on, and tend to treat thrown objects with indifference or even disdain. They will see the object fall and their ears will prick up with the prospect of something to chase, and they may even race forward to examine the object, but the interest ends there. Thus it is literally imperative to teach a lurcher with a strong dash of sight-hound blood the skill of retrieving while it is still very young before it has entered the indifferent or blasé stage, so to speak.

One of the commonest faults made when training a dog to retrieve is to attempt to train it in the presence of another dog. Once one has started this training practice, it is almost impossible to get a dog to deliver an object to hand. I'll explain why. The dog is taken out with another dog, and an object, a fur dummy, a ball (it matters not what), is thrown. The dog about to retrieve is exhilarated and races forward, picks up the object and returns to the owner who is crouched to make the prospect of retrieving even more interesting, for few dogs fail to find a person crouched into an unusual shape anything other than fascinating. The dog returns to the owner at a gallop, only to find another dog on a leash, ready and more than willing to take the prize from the would-be retriever. Thus the dog returning with the dummy becomes chary of giving up its treasure even to its owner, and circles the man with the dog on the leash. Now, this is an annoying fault, and the man is irritated, justifiably, one may think, until one examines why the dog is behaving thus. It is an incredibly clever man who can conceal his annoyance from a dog. The dog picks up the vibrations from the man, becomes bewildered, frightened, and instantly the task ceases to be a game, and the potentially useful lurcher degenerates to a sight hound eager to run and catch its prey but reluctant to retrieve it.

Merle puppy

A lurcher trainer needs to train one dog at a time if he is to succeed, but just as an athlete needs a pacer to keep him at the top of his form, just as Bannister needed Chataway to enable him to crash through his four-minute mile record, so does a trainer require a pacer to ensure that he pushes his dog to the limits of sensible training. If one is alone while training a dog, the chances are that one becomes complacent about the results, satisfied with less than the dog could have done perhaps, prepared to accept that one's goose is really a swan, so to speak.

As luck would have it, my own pacer turned up on my doorstep just three weeks after Merle had arrived. I was working on the book *Adventures of an Artisan Hunter* at the time, and deeply engrossed in tidying up the text. Not the easiest of tasks, for I'm a messy worker, to say the least. A car pulled up and I groaned aloud, for that day my phone had been red hot with a spate of fools asking, 'Can you get me a deerhound – greyhound – saluki – collie – borzoi – greyhound (genuine) just ready for starting work?' Boy, I love these people.

My caller, however, was one Tony Aherne, a pit electrician, who did not want a dog, for he'd just bought one, but was interested in buying a copy of my earlier books, *Rogues and Running Dogs*. With him was a heavy mastiff-fat puppy, a collie greyhound like Merle, some four weeks older and bred by mating a collie dog to a black track greyhound bitch. Terry was not particularly happy about his purchase and was casting appreciative not to say fond and envying glances at a deerhoundy litter I had just bred, wirey-coated, elegant greyhoundy puppies – in fact, everyone's idea of what a lurcher should be. Yet his puppy was bright, frantic to please, eager to perform and obviously intelligent – in fact, my idea of what a lurcher should be, and indeed what I was trying to create.

'Do you sell these?' He nodded towards the radiantly elegant Snowball, a curious name for a brown, long-coated lurcher.

'Trying to breed them out,' I replied, probably sound a bit blasé.

His puzzled face indicated that he needed an explanation, and after I had explained I fetched Merle out of the house. I had expected approval, but Terry winced.

'Jesus,' he said, 'and I thought mine was ugly'.

In spite of such an inauspicious start, we became firm friends from that day forth, and Terry's training of Rusty, as he called the puppy, paced that of my own dog.

Despite their similar breeding, both being collie greyhound first crosses, the pups were as different as chalk from cheese. Terry's puppy grew into a heavy dog, heavier even than Merle, and so heavy that few lurcher breeders who had not seen his elegant, fast progeny

Tony Aherne and Rusty

would have been tempted to use him as a stud. Rusty was an extrovert, a boisterous sycophant of a dog, much attached to children and willing to allow any indignity at the hands of Terry's three kids. Merle detested small children, and for that matter so do I. Perhaps my thinking, my attitude towards such kids therefore conditioned the dog to dislike youngsters. Furthermore, Merle is inclined to be sullen with strangers, unwilling to come to people he does not know intimately, but again this might be due to the later events that shaped his life – but I must not run ahead of my tale.

Terry's dog was perhaps easier to train because of his ebullient nature. If he was hurt during training, he recovered his nerve quickly. A mobile jumping frame once fell on him, winding and terrifying him, yet minutes later he was jumping again. This same treatment would have finished Merle, rendered him untrainable for days, unwilling to try such a jump for weeks. Likewise, an injury sustained during a retrieving session rendered Merle reluctant to try the retrieve again, yet an identical injury sustained by Terry's dog was forgotten in moments. Merle was more wary of people, perhaps, but as he grew older he became fiercely aggressive with any dog that menaced him, willing to pursue a conflict to its bloody conclusion should a dog upset him. Rusty, however, rarely became involved in skirmishes, even when terribly menaced. Both became excellent jumpers, capable of seven-foot leaps, both had excellent noses, and it would be difficult to decide which of the two was the more intelligent. Most importantly, both were a joy to train, possessing true collie delight in doing any task, no matter how complex or odious, providing it pleased the trainer. Neither were fast dogs, capable of effortless flowing courses at hares, though both would try until their hearts burst, but that, again, is a quality most collies seem to have.

Throughout that summer, Terry in Tamworth and DBP some five miles away spent their waking hours training the two puppies, comparing progress each day, each one no doubt secretly seeking to better the other's attainment. It was an unfair contest, for not only was I fifteen years older than Terry, but my life had been spent training dogs of this ilk, and I was fairly certain that I would defeat Terry in the training stakes, that I'd take my puppy well beyond the limit of Terry's dog's achievements, but then I had reckoned without the interference of Vampire.

3 Vampire

'He's a poisonous little sod,' said Alex. 'Dead game, I'll give you that, but poisonous. Personally, if he were mine (and I'm glad he isn't) I'd say he'd need balancing.' My raised eyebrow indicated that I hadn't understood, so he proceeded. 'Yeh, he needs a tiny piece of lead placed in his left ear'ole,' he added philosophically, like a medieval physician prescribing a witchcraft remedy for a curious mental condition.

'How do I put it there?' I asked, thoroughly mystified by the treatment.

'With a bloody twelve bore,' Alex exploded, aiming a kick at the dog, who avoided Alex's geriatric attack but continued to circle the old chap, snarling like a fiend, lips lifted to reveal an overlong set of carnassial teeth.

Alex lifted his bleeding fell terrier bitch above his head in readiness for Vampire's next attack. 'She only went near his bloody sheep's head and he did this' – he nodded his head at the lacerated bitch, still spouting blood from half a dozen deep rips. 'Bastard,' he added, aiming another kick, but Vampire continued to circle him, roaring softly like a demented creature, his eyes glazed with fury.

I suppose I must put most of the blame on myself, for I had bred Vampire, deliberately created him, so to speak. My old terrier bloodlines was running a bit fine, and I had resorted to close inbreeding, a practice that all but finished my kennels. The inbred line had courage right enough, and nose too, better nose than my present stock, but each litter was dotted with deformed puppies. Hydrocephalic puppies, tiny mites with huge domed heads resembling the Mekon of Dan Dare, were found in most litters, but the domed skull was full of watery fluid not brain, and by the age of ten weeks most were blind, subject to fits and without a sense of balance. One half of my puppies were born with cleft palates, which in layman's terms meant no roof to the mouth – a condition that prevented them from suckling and ensured that, within three days of being born, they had bleated themselves into emaciated, dehydrated little corpses. I needed outcross blood, two or three generations of new blood, to

Vampire

Some of Vampire's progeny, among the best hunting dogs I own

correct these maladies, so Vampire was 'created'. Come to think of it, I may have been better off putting up with the inherent weakness of the strain, the cleft palate and the hydrocephaly, for Vampire, true to his name, was a heller. Except that he was, to quote Mo, 'the most even-tempered of dogs', for Vampire was *always* nasty.

Although I'd contemplated using various stud dogs to revive my flagging, inbred strain, there simply weren't any really suitable males about. I'd go to a show, see a classy well-worked male terrier, ask its proud owner if it was worked, receive an incredible, and undoubtedly exaggerated, account of the dog's hunting prowess, and settle down quite happily about using the terrier. I'd add a quick, 'What's he bred from?' and the tale would change. 'From a very good dog,' would be the answer, but which dog he didn't know. Seemingly all Jack Russells are bred from 'a very good terrier'. There just weren't any suitable dogs to bring into my strain, for to bring in a 'pedigree unknown dog' to an inbred strain of dog is courting disaster. Irony of ironies, I finally settled for a stud dog that had never seen legitimate work and wasn't even a true terrier.

I didn't know Jem Hackett all that well, and frankly, my lack of social contact with him didn't worry me all that much. To use a cliché, Jem and I 'weren't the same type'. In fact, I've never really had much of an affection for the dog-fighting fraternity. For the hell of me I can't understand why any man should spend hours of time, love and affection rearing a puppy only to see it fight to the death or receive crippling wounds at the jaws of another dog. No, Hackett wasn't my sort of person, but he owned a veritable cyclone of a dog which he called Tarka, but which was known to the dog-fighting set as the Hackett White.

Most of the strains of Stafford are what is known in pit parlance as 'spent'. In other words, the raw diabolical courage, the insane desire to rip, rend and destroy has been bred out in favour of more beefy, placid-tempered dogs capable of winning in the shows rather than in the pits. Hackett didn't keep that sort of dog. His dogs were the old type, fast, racy terrierish in type, scarcely thirty pounds in weight, not at all suitable for Kennel Club shows, but what they lacked in body weight they made up in blind courage. The White, for people simply called him that, was a maniac, a devil incarnate, for whenever he bit through the chain link fence in Hackett's builder's yard, he could easily be tracked by following the trail of carnage. Cats, dogs, horses, pigs were all grist to his ferocious mill, and story has it that he once attacked a circus elephant. It seemed a bit far fetched when Hackett told me, until Farley explained that Hackett had taken the demented dog to the circus to see if it would back down from 'a big un'. I've never seen a gamer dog, and I'll leave it at that, except to add that Hackett certainly wasn't as courageous and simply kept the brute as an image creator. The White's daughters were, on the other hand, as unlike their father as chalk to cheese.

Against much advice, I took Thistle, a really game little terrier of my own strain, to be mated to the demon dog, and she produced a litter of three bitches, all of which I gave away because they were too soft. Frankly, I'd seen poodles with more assertive qualities than Jennie, the biggest bitch, so I gave her as a present to Audrey Taylor, a twelve-year-old daughter of a friend. Tim Corrington, the old-time dog fighter, consort of Cockney Charlie Lloyd, once told me that fighting blood didn't die out, it simply slumbered, even missed a generation or so until the correct ingredient was added to the crucible – then a very heller emerged from the mixture. In due time, Audrey brought back her bitch to be served, and I mated her to Laddie, a dog I had purchased from the Chiddingford and Leconfield Hunt. The correct ingredient had been added to the crucible, though, on reflection, 'correct' seems questionable. I took one look at the litter and bought all back at £20 a piece – a hell of a price to pay for a Russell type of puppy twelve years ago when decent show puppies could be bought for a tenner. Vampire, Witch, Warlock and Verdelak – incredible names for incredible dogs. Vampire is still with me, a crochety, violent old man, stiff, sore and tired after every hunt. The rest are no longer with me – Vampire killed all three of them, for, to quote Alex, Vampire was, and is, 'a poisonous little sod'.

Puppies, however, are puppies, and evil disposition does not manifest itself until a dog is at least five months old. My veteran San was senile by then, and signs of social discontent were ripplying through the pack with a number of males vying for the No. 1 position shortly to be vacated. Perhaps this discontent, this electrically charged atmosphere, helped in distorting Vampire, or perhaps the spirit of the Hackett White had slumbered long enough and now, like the Kraken, was about to stir. I'd had portents of the forthcoming battle, rumblings so to speak, but it was not to be the run-of-the-mill skirmish, the stupid day-to-day, bickering, spiteful battle I'd expected. Pack fights are serious, particularly unattended pack fights. Battles in hound kennels left unattended or unstopped invariably end in a death or so and a bad atmosphere for weeks following. Terrier fights are worse, a million times worse, for no more persistent and aggressive type of dog exists. Blows, shouting, water will usually break up hound battles, but they only serve to increase the fury of terriers involved in a fight.

My own fight broke out over nothing when I was exercising my terrier pack in the run one Saturday afternoon. Vanity menaced Vogue – her sister, actually – over some trifle, and all hell broke loose with one huge mêlée of thirty wrestling dogs in the middle of the run and six or seven minor but very bloody battles taking place all over the place. I clubbed, kicked and kennelled up as fast as I could all the bitches I could lay hands or feet on, only to find that Laddie had set about the six-month-old Vampire, seemingly for no reason at all. I grabbed both the grapplers, threw them into Barlow's field, and resumed my struggle separating the combatants. An hour later, bleeding, bitter, exhausted and bruised, I was still trying to stop the main fight.

To cut a long story short, I had three dogs die as a result of that fight, two bitches and a dog to be precise, and I was cleaning up the survivors when I remembered the battle taking place in Barlow's field. 'My God,' I panicked, 'they've been at it for three hours.' I jumped the fence. They were still fighting, panting, snarling, their breath coming in sobbing snorts through bloody, lacerated nostrils. Laddie was a hell of a mess, one ear torn nearly off, a bad groin bite leaking blood and filth, his face swollen until he looked like a bull terrier. Vampire was also damaged, but each bite, each puncture, had only served to infuriate him all the more. I separated them and my hand came within reach of the enraged Vampire. Curiously, I felt little pain, more of a sense of amazement of hearing my bones crack and splinter under that awful crushing bite. It was a full five minutes before I could strangle the fiend off from my hand. Laddie stood there, dripping blood and swaying like an aspen, but Vampire had, to use an Americanism, 'finally flipped'. My fingers never really healed straight through that encounter, and I had a hell of a job explaining to a Jamaican doctor at casualty why my legs and back were also severely punctured. But, after that fight, only the most foolhardy of the dogs challenged Vampire, and even the bitches, favourite bitches of his, gave him a clear berth during exercise period in the run.

Most dogs, in fact most creatures, look on attack as the last resort, the ultimate action, after all bluff or attempts at assertion have been tried and failed. A roaring rumble will usually preceed a lip-raising session that is fairly certain to put the fear of God into any subordinate animal, particularly a young puppy. If this fails, a dog will cause his face to crease with rage and even chance a snap or so at an adversary, making sure not one of the bites connects, of course. Only when this has failed will he finally resort to serious attack. The fights beloved of Jack London, the systematic, well-thought-out fights for leadership, just don't take place, and for damn good reason. Any pack of dogs which behave like those Yukon dogs of fiction would be non-functional or extinct within weeks. Bluff plays a very important part in the struggle for leadership, and it is only when the bluff fails that serious battles take place. Even then, the battles are usually fairly minor affairs, and as soon as supremacy has been established, the vanquished slinks away or finds something else to do, and the victor, still strutting, bristling and snarling, refuses to follow.

Vampire was dangerous, a biological time bomb, for he did not conform to the accepted social codes of canine behaviour. Some dog (or bitch, he finally killed nine terrier bitches through battles started by him) would upset him, and straight away, without any prepartory behaviour or ritual, he would attack, and singularly inoffensive actions seemed to infuriate him. Most of the dogs simply avoided him or attended to other things when approached by him, but the most frightening aspect was the fact that he would attack young and old alike, not heeding even the submissive responses of puppies.

His grip was astounding and none of the panaceas regarding making a dog release its hold seemed to work with him. He would lunge, grip, lock, and neither choking him nor doing something unmentionable to his genitals would cause him to release his hold. Why I kept a dog of this character must be a puzzle to the reader, but on the other side of the scales was the fact that his courage was bottomless, his nose unerring. Last but by no means least, he fathered offspring like Omega, my ultimate rat killer. Frankly, although I cursed him a hundred times a day, I simply couldn't afford to get rid of him. Moses, cryptic as ever, came out with the last word on the subject. 'Every dog has his place,' he said, eyeing Vampire intimidating all and sundry. 'I'll go and dig his, if you like!'

I should like to be able to describe a mounting tension between victim and aggressor, Fitzpatrick style, leading up to what happened next, but that was not the way it was. I had taken Merle into the run and allowed him to socialize with the mad mêlée of young terriers, who were amazed but not frightened by the size of the infant plodding among them. Then something made me turn my head, and out of the corner of my eye I saw Vampire flash through the air at the puppy – no reason or logic, and certainly no threat had triggered off the attack. I saw the puppy literally bowled off its feet, with Vampire latched to its foreleg. Then all hell broke loose, with a dozen half-crazed terriers, all half-brothers, sisters and daughters of the old murderer's, ripping and tearing at the poor devil on the floor. I kicked, beat and flung the offenders into Barlow's field (a spot that, when an estate is finally built there, will echo with the ghostly sounds of falling canines) until only Vampire hung on, gritting his teeth, his eyes glazing with an insane glow, his face taking on an ecstatic look.

His teeth were firmly embedded in the foreleg of the puppy and the jaws were macerating the flesh. I wrapped binder twine around Vamp's neck, and using it as a tourniquet began to strangle him. His roaring took on a frenzied note which petered out into a sort of sob as, swaying on his feet, he released his awful hold.

Merle lay there unmoving, unblinking, eyes staring at nothing, his body soaked in blood, filth and urine. Once, with an almost mechanical movement, he tried to rise, only to fall back again, voiding the contents of his stomach and bowels. He was bleeding from a dozen wounds, his foreleg dreadfully macerated, a deep bite (the result of Beltane, Vampire's equally ferocious sister) in his belly, from which seeped an unpleasant greeny-brown fluid. He was all but dead before I reached my vet's house.

Meanwhile, Vampire raged in his kennel, jumping at the bars, frantic to be in at the kill of the stricken puppy. He continued to rage well into evening, pulling at the wires until his mouth bled, frenzied at being denied his kill. Later that evening, he tore open his cage and killed Blaze, his red and white daughter. For once I seriously considered Alex's suggestion that I balanced Vampire – with the tiny piece of shot in his ear.

4 An Incomplete Lurcher

I must leap ahead in my tale now, partly because it is expedient to do
so, partly because few people are interested in the tale of the
recuperation of an injured dog, but mostly because the days of his
convalescence were unhappy days and my mind tends to shut out
unhappy times (and God knows, there have been enough of those in
my wretched career). Merle had been my *raison d'être* for months, he
had been my thoughts in waking and sleeping, and subsequently my
mind had blotted out the misery of my everyday professional teaching
life, of the back-biting, the childish spitefulness that only adults who
work in a child-oriented world can perpetrate. Now, with Merle *hors
de combat*, hideously macerated, maybe even crippled, the prospects
looked bleak. Not only had I wasted months of training, but now the
full unhappiness of my everyday life became apparent. Part of my
success in the training of Merle, getting him to a standard of
obedience that revived my faith in the truth of Brian Vesey-
FitzGerald's tales of tinker-trained lurchers, had been due to the fact
that I needed to have some success in something. I was a hopeless
failure at my job, so I put all my efforts, all my aspirations, into the
training of this ugly little dog. Every man needs to succeed at
something, to find he is good at some task, to make life worth living.
The full force of my sense of failure hit me the day after Merle's
dreadful mangling, and my diary for that time reads like an Edgar
Allan Poe poem. Thus I will gloss over it all and leap ahead a month
or so.

Just before Holkham Fair, a spectacular show on the east coast of
England worth attending if only for the multi-faceted characters who
throng to it, Merle had completely recovered. Even his slight limp
had left him, to return only on days when he thought he had offended
me. On a day during that week of Holkham Fair, Merle came upon
his first rabbit, a youngster still green, a little off territory, perhaps.
Irony of ironies, Merle ran and caught that first rabbit, the first live
rabbit he had ever seen. I say irony of ironies, because in spite of what
country books, usually written by retired generals living in the wilds
of Chiswick, say, the rabbit is an extraordinarily difficult creature to

'Most feed close up to the hedges during the day-time . . .'

catch. Most feed close up to the hedges during the day-time and hop
back to safety when threatened. Most know the runs back to their
burrows like the backs of their paws. Their very survival depends on
it, and they instinctively follow this well-worn route when any hassle
seems likely.

Yet Merle caught his first rabbit. It had myxomatosis as it
happened, but it was a catch nevertheless, though he trapped it
between his paws before retrieving it. It is curious, but most collie
crosses tend to start catching by dint of using their paws to hold the
rabbit. Even so, it was to be weeks before he took another, partly
beause the rabbit really does take some catching, and partly because
that first indication of myxomatosis marked the end of my rabbit
population.

A rabbiting dog, a dog skilled at taking rabbits, is an amalgam of
many qualities, though funnily enough such a dog is not prized by

'Few courses after rabbits are longer than fifty yards . . .'

lurcher men as highly as a dog which can take hare. First, a rabbit-hunting dog needs to be quick off the mark, not necessarily blindingly fast over a grinding two-mile course or endowed with enough stamina to run all day. Few courses after rabbits are longer than fifty yards during daylight hours, for few rabbits feed more than fifty yards from home. What is needed is what is known as an 'instant' mind, a mind that can see a chance, snatch up that chance and make a quick lunge that will finish up with a rabbit. The whippet mentality, particularly the fiery track whippets of the north, whose ancestry is peppered with terrier blood, is ideal for the job, while the larger deerhound types of lurcher, elegant and fast, are not usually as well suited to the job of rabbiting.

Fathom is an ace at rabbiting, and has been since she ceased to be a puppy. At twenty-three inches at the shoulder – scarcely bigger than an outsized whippet, the size I consider ideal for a lurcher – she is just about the job for the cut-and-thrust task of rabbiting. Furthermore, she is capable of a very crafty stalk, half belly to ground, half crouch, inching forward before she decides to make her bid. To say, in true romantic fashion, that her aim and her final thrust is unnerving would be stretching it a bit, but she is still a remarkably accurate striker. She is also seven months older than Merle, and though the age difference seems ridiculous now both are veterans, it was once an enormous chasm, a chasm that tended to convince me that Merle, for all his canine IQ, was far from what I wanted.

She could always beat him to the punch, no matter how hard he tried – and no dog tried harder during the first autumn which preceeded his first eventful and character-forming winter. Fathom would see a rabbit at the same time as Merle, and both would try for it, Merle always getting there first, for in spite of his unlurcher-like shape, Fathom could not live with him during a fair course. But you could bet your bottom dollar that it was Fathom's head that came up, rabbit in jaws. After a while, Merle refused to try when he was out at exercise with Fathom, and would rather unhappily watch her course and retrieve her kill just a yard or so away, tantalizingly circling just out of hand's reach, for she was unhappy about sharing her catch with another dog. Thus I took to exercising him by himself, but such was his lack of agility or lack of the 'instant' sort of mind that is so essential in a rabbiting dog that he never really made the grade as a daytime rabbiter. He would catch well enough, but somehow he lacked that certain something which Fathom possessed.

I stress daytime rabbiter. For work after dark, pursuing a rabbit illuminated by a beam of light in the sport called lamping, a somewhat different type of dog is often required. No less dexterous a dog or agile a lurcher, but one even more so, perhaps, for to perform the near acrobatics required to catch rabbits along a narrow beam of light over irregular surfaced fields through winter-blackened thistles requires a somewhat extraordinary type of canine intelligence. It is, however, often easier to start a dog at rabbiting on the lamp, for rabbits will feed quite a way from a warren when they have the protection of darkness. Thus not only does a dog have a chance of a longer run, albeit a run conducted under more perilous circumstances than during daylight hours, but rabbits illuminated by a beam of light sometimes squat and refuse to run in the mistaken idea that they are not visible if they keep perfectly still. But no matter how tight a rabbit sits, his eyes still shine like rubies in the light of the beam. Even so, it often requires a skilled and experienced lurcher to pick up squatters that refuse to move until the lamper can actually touch them with his feet. Some lurchers never learn to catch these rabbits until the squatter can be persuaded to move.

Both Fathom and Merle began lamping that same winter, and both took to it as easily as if they had been born to it. Merle was kept on the slip that first night, but henceforth he remained obediently at heel, or during his later life crouched behind me as we waited for heavier quarry than rabbits to appear in the beam. He never became the perfect, complete lurcher, skilled at all forms of hunting from lamping to net work, but he became a competent lamping dog. He might have become a more than competent lamping dog had not a curious event actually altered the course of his life. I have always boasted that I have a quick mind and am capable of very dexterous sleight of hand, but a matter of two weeks after Merle began lamping, I was to be taken in by a very much more skilful sleight of hand, the greatest confidence trick of them all − the *hokano baro*.

5 Hokano Baro

Autumn drifted into winter and one morning I crossed the fields before light – before respectable people are abroad, my mother used to say, to try to stop my nocturnal wanderings – only to find the top end of the lane literally strewn with caravans, bright chrome lorry-drawn affairs that somehow or other sleep an incredible number of people and often house a multitude of sins. Ten years before the police had raided such caravans, parked in a rather snooty area of fashionable Lichfield, and after a search uncovered some twelve terriers secreted and stowed away like crockery, for travelling folk have great skill in packing away bulky objects in small spaces. Mind you, six of the terriers did not survive the hasty packaging that preceded the raid and died within hours of their unpacking, but this is an unimportant detail so far as the reader is concerned. It was, at the time, rather more important to me since they were my terriers, but that is another tale.

I'm not automatically against itinerants, dubbing them all thieves, calling them all undesirably filthy. Many travellers, Romanies, tinkers and so forth, are not only no trouble at all but are also extremely clean. Moses Smith, my closest friend, and George Gaskin, from one of the most famous gipsy families, must rank as the most hygiene-conscious people I've ever known (and come to think of it, I'm building a horse-drawn vardo as I write this book and planning to go on the road myself as soon as I am made redundant). But having said all that, some of the travellers I've met are literally disgusting.

When I came to this area in the mid 1960s I befriended Ephraim, a strange sort of chap by any standards, and he gave me a piece of advice, one of those pearls of wisdom that must be classed among the epigrams of life. Ephraim, a *didikai* himself, would camp maybe two miles away and walk to my shack each day. When I suggested his moving nearer, to the edge of my tangleweed-filled garden, he declined. 'Doing yer a favour living out,' he lisped. 'If I go there and stay more 'an a day, the rest'll see it's place suitable for a site, and you'll be bogged in tinkers.' Funnily enough, he proved correct.

Gipsies and tinkers are inveterate sign followers, and certain signs tell passing itinerants the way a district treats similar vagrants, and since I intend a spell of horse-drawn vagrancy myself, it is expedient for me to have made a study of these signs. A single hearth with little trampling of the ground around the fire means the district is hostile to travellers, and that within minutes of their arrival, the council will have served a 'move on in seventy-two hours' notice. Likewise, much wear of grass and a lot of use of the hearth means the council are a bit 'couldn't care less' and it's an open invitation for travellers to settle. George Gaskin, at seventy-four, settled temporarily in Grantham, but, with a decided nostalgia for the road, usually avoided settling near a rubbish-strewn temporary site, as not only was such a district a health hazard, but the people who had strewn the rubbish were usually a bit antipathetic, to say the least (violent would be more accurate), to persons other than their own families.

Our own tinker invasion – and in a district the size of our hamlet 'invasion' just about sums it up – started when the tinkers decided to settle in a very posh district of Lichfield, and as quickly as they were moved on another band came. A week later by an amazing co-incidence – the council assure us it was nothing more, and councils are never known to lie, are they? – the trees along our lane were cut down and the land levelled. I don't live in a very posh area and few influential people inhabit our village. This, too, is a coincidence I suppose. Within a month of the havoc in our lane, we had tinkers, and Ephraim, who came that autumn, shook his head in sorrow and predicted the worst – except that it was worse than Ephraim predicted. Much worse. 'Put in a complaint as soon as the first band arrive,' he suggested, and had we listened perhaps we would have come off lightly. As it was, we had no cause to complain at the outset. Our first visitors were called Frank and family, a genial Irish tinker whose sons were respectful and no real trouble. Their dogs killed a cat, and the boys poached the land, but this was small beer compared to the horror to come. No one disliked Frank, and no one objected to his two-month stay. Frank's friends who came just as Frank and family decided to leave were not quite as pleasant, though, and not quite as tidy either, and not only were a few objects, spades, wheelbarrows and so on missing when the band left the district, but there was a considerable pile of rubbish left in their wake as well. Well, we sighed, thanked God that they'd left, and prayed we'd seen an end to them, and when Frank and family returned, we weren't quite as friendly as we'd been before.

Frank stayed maybe a month this time, causing no offence and no trouble, and we'd just about got over the tinker hurt when Frank

George Gaskin

upped sticks and left. It was as if he'd received some premonition, some warning of the hell to follow, and after Frank left the hell began. I crossed the fields that morning with Snowball, a beautiful brown, rough-coated bitch, whose photograph is opposite the flyleaf of *The Complete Lurcher*, in company with Merle and Fathom, whose hind leg had festered through a nail injury – a wound I cursed at the time, but which was later to prove her salvation. Then I came upon the caravans, twenty-five of them, enough caravans to house a horde of tinkers – 125 of them to be exact. For the next month the village was under siege. I can remember groaning aloud at the sight of them, knowing that my house, being left unattended during the days, would be a No. 1 target once these people had looked the district over. Manfri Woods, in his book *In the Life of a Romany Gypsy*, states that gipsies don't go for a walk to while away the time. If they are on foot, they are looking the district over for poaching potential or future stealing. It was small consolation to know this when I found hordes drifting past my window, and when I arrived home that evening, my log pile, the result of six back-breaking, freezing days at the fallen trees in the near-by wood, had vanished.

That week I turned on my fast-flickering TV and saw a representative of the Tinker Council speaking about how he just couldn't understand why villages didn't welcome travellers. The same day, the band stripped a local combine harvester and sold it for scrap, stole numerous hens, used one of the local houses, vacant while under renovation, as a toilet, daubing their filth over the walls. When the house was nailed up – few people in the district used to lock their doors even at night at one time – they tipped their unmentionable filth in the ditch, where it stank to high heaven and attracted hordes of rats that came from miles around to feed on the growing pile of garbage and filth. The same week my game fowl, black reds that had cost me a fortune in hard-earned money, disappeared. Frankly, where tinkers are concerned, there is nothing a householder can do to protect his property.

The law, far from discriminating against tinkers, has its hands tied by misguided well wishers who wish to protect tinker villains. If a tinker is picked up for a crime in this district, he invariably gives his name as, 'James Brown, sir,' goes to magistrate's court, obtains bail and hops it, for magistrates, badgered by solicitors who wish to make a name for themselves (and a hell of a lot of loot, for nearly all itinerants, rich as Croesus and poor alike, obtain legal aid) as defenders of the rights of minorities, will release a tinker on bail rather than chance an allegation of discrimination against itinerants. Staffordshire abounds with such solicitors, eagerly pushing for greater rights for tinkers but living in some ritzy part of town well away from a tinker site, its garbage, its violence, its aggression.

Say, how about fame! A mathematical law named after me: Plummer's Law. *A person's enthusiasm for tinkers is in direct proportion to the miles he lives from a tinker site.* Sounds high falutin', but it's accurate, believe me. People who are interested in traveller's rights invariably live a long way from any site. Hence, few police are keen to do much about tinker damage, and don't exactly go out of their way to obtain an arrest, for they know that as soon as the court case comes up, they will be standing around the waiting rooms like lemons waiting for a case that won't be heard, for James Brown will be miles away, probably using the summons as toilet paper. I'm neither pro-police nor anti-itinerant – as I've said, I intend to go on the road myself – but legislation needs to be strengthened to ensure the countryside isn't terrorized by such bands as visited our lane that dreadful month.

A chronicle recording the appearance of the first gipsies ever to visit France reads, 'They eat like starving pigs. They are disgusting in their private habits. They stink and are full of vermin.' That just about described the crowd at the end of my lane. The stench from the midden pile was ghastly and the headlights of oncoming cars illuminated hordes of rats feeding on the filth. A few days after the departure of the band, some lads ferreted and killed fifty-four rats from the hedge near the filth pile, but I jump my tale again.

Now, I may be conceited, but up until then I thought I was a moderately, not extremely, mind you, intelligent chap. I speak quite a few Asiatic languages, have a reasonably articulate if vitriolic tongue, am able to work out the readings on my electricity meter fairly well, and even understand the occasional council edict. Thus it was infuriating that, towards the end of the tinker month of hell, I should be taken by the oldest trick in the book, a variation on a theme maybe, but still the oldest trick in the Romany book – the *hokano baro*, a trick a Romany child would laugh at. And it was a child that sold me the trick, damn him.

Traditionally, the *hokano baro*, in English 'the great trick', is practised on gullible country bumpkins, so I could kick myself for not spotting it coming, and furthermore I felt a damned idiot, reporting it to the young bobby who, young as he was, with a cherubic face and unjaundiced views on life, spotted the con trick as soon as I told him about it. First, I'll explain the traditional *hokano baro*. A gipsy rolls up to a house of an obviously well-to-do person (in my case it was clearly a variation on a theme, for I'm always on my uppers moneywise) and sells his or her *schpiel*. Traditionally, the *hokano baro* is played by a woman, who is usually more persuasive than a man, though in my case it was a child. Woman knocks on door, begs or 'duckers' (tells fortunes), then sniffs the air curiously. 'There's gold buried in the house, deary, gold trapped by a spell.' The bumpkin gazes back in wonder, mouth open, and the trap is set, ready to be sprung. Bumpkin asks how the gipsy knows, and is told Romanies have a nose for gold (which, brother, in the case of the tale to come is probably the only truthful statement). 'Only one thing to do,' says the Romany, who has performed a few conjuring tricks to impress the *gaujo* (which in Romany terms is not only synonymous with 'outsider', but actually can be used to mean 'clodhopper' or 'sucker'). 'You must gather the goods of value, gold, silver, the like, place it in a bundle made of this cloth' – cloth appears from jacket as if by magic (I just happen to have brought my music along) – and leave it for three weeks, for it is a known fact that gold attracts gold.'

Now only a lunatic or a self-opinionated, Romany-speaking school-teacher would go for this rubbish – the gold strolling out of the brickwork to join its friends in the pile under the cloth, but a number of idiots have gone for it. So clodhopper races away, gathers up all his treasured possessions, wedding rings, christening candlesticks, the lot, and places them beneath the cloth in the darkest part of the cellar to wait for the maverick gold to join it. After three weeks with occasional peeps at the bundle, his enthusiasm made greater by a gold coin which has clearly inched its way out of the masonry to join its mates under the cloth, he whips off the cloth to find that his gold pieces, his rings, his jewellery, his christening candlesticks have all changed, as if by magic, to brass washers and iron blocks. To his utter amazement, the gipsy band has also vanished. Still, that's magic, I guess. Some you win, some you lose. Amazed, dear reader, how anyone could be stupid enough to go for this load of hogwash, startled at this extraordinary instance of gross credulity? Well, hundreds of suckers were milked by this trick or by a hundred or so variations on the theme. Brian Vesey-FitzGerald says that the last instance of classic *hokano baro* took place in 1937 – a good year for vintage suckers, it seems, for I was born in the September of that year, and some forty or so later became victim of the trick.

Hell, how could I be taken by such a ploy? I am amazed, ashamed and mystified by my own incredible credulity, and to have had the *ryke* pulled by a ten-year-old child is doubly embarrassing. I arrived home from school that day to find a rather ragged but innocent-looking tinker child holding one of my terriers and waiting in my porch.

'Sir, der leetle dog was running loose, sir.'

Always 'sir', the tinker equivalent of *gorgio* no doubt.
'Best check to see if any of de others is out.'

Heart in my mouth, I raced up to the run, passing the terrier kennels to check at where Merle, Snowball and Fathom (still festering) were kennelled. I breathed a sigh of relief and then rather half-heartedly checked the other less valuable dogs. Nothing was missing, and I fell against the shed exhausted but grateful. It was only then that I noticed the tinker child had followed me into the run and was watching me with an almost casual air. I'd love to be able to say that in true Perry Mason fashion I smelt a rat instantly, but I didn't, and out of gratitude gave the lad a pound, my last pound, and then had to scratch around the house for coppers to buy milk. But the stage was set for *hokano baro*. I'd fallen for it, taken the bait, hook, line and sinker.

I had forty-five dogs – too many for a tinker to steal, and too many to test the value of each and every dog in turn before stealing the valuable ones. They now had no need to check which dog was the best, however. I'd done it for them. My anxiety at having my dogs missing had made me race up the run and check the dogs I valued most. Next night Merle and Snowball were missing and the travellers gone (Fathom was at the vet's, in danger of losing a leg). Classic *hokano baro*, led smack bang into it by a ten-year-old unlettered, illiterate child. How hath the mighty fallen (Kings 11)? But even then I was too stupid to see what had happened, too pompous to accept the truth, too proud to admit I'd been conned. I phoned the police, and rang Mo while the police were arriving, telling Mo about the theft.

'Did you have a fore visit?' he asked. I told him, and he roared with laughter. 'It's the oldest one in the world, you idiot, you idiot,' he repeated, roaring with laughter.

He didn't need to say any more. The penny had dropped. I felt a knot in my gut, a mixture of anger, despair and humiliation.

Reader, forget trying to recover dogs stolen by itinerants. You're wasting your time. Drive around any and every tinker camp in the country, get search warrants if you can or have time enough to waste. You won't find anything. You'll uncover a host of other things, ranging from illegal guns to cocker spaniels, perhaps, which may please the police and clear up a few cases, but it won't do you much good. Itinerant thieves are usually avoided by honest God-fearing Romanies, but these thieves know every drop in the country, every settled itinerant or *kerengro* from those living in rabbit-warren, council-house estates, to *nouveau riche* owners of farms and country houses, and quite a few of them are ready to accept a 'drop', an animal recently stolen that is valuable enough though 'hot'. Sit on your backside and wait, was Ephraim's advice, and maybe offer up a prayer to St Sarah, the patron saint of Romanies. But I was in no mood for comments of this nature, for I had never experienced such bitterness and hatred.

I had spent months working on Merle, and if he was not my ideal lurcher, he was as near as dammit is to swearing to what I wanted. For eight long and tedious months I had trained him, trained him to an amazing standard of obedience, I had thought: encourged him to be suspicious of strangers, wary of anyone new; taught him to accept food only when I offered it. He was not a great rabbiting dog, and certainly no hare dog of a type that would appeal to these people, but they had sensed his value to me, misunderstood his personal value, confused it with cash value, considered that what I considered valuable they would consider of worth. He was an experiment, a chance to see how far I could take a sight-hound blooded dog, maybe the start of a pedigree of lurchers. Useful, intelligent lurchers, the start of a dynasty perhaps, but they had stolen him simply because I had considered him valuable.

I put out a description: height, 23 inches; colour, merle; white eye patch; weight 55 lb (I'd weighed him two days previously), but I had little chance of recovering him. Curiously, although Snowball, my beautiful hare courser, my Lambourn winner, my most perfect physical specimen, was also stolen, this didn't seem to worry me very much. She was classy enough to change hands for a good sum, find a home in some wealthy *kerengro*'s kennel, have a good life coursing hares twice a week, but Merle, what in hell would happen to my ugly, shy and brilliant dog after they had found he was 'funny' with strangers, not really a good hare dog, realized that his colour made him so conspicuous that no one would buy him, and the only way of disposing of him was to sink him with concrete in a near-by canal? I felt sick with worry.

I sat there in my untidy house upon my rocking chair, gripping my knees and rocking to and fro like something out of *One Flew Over the Cuckoo's Nest*, deep in thought and swearing vengeance on the band.

'Can you prove it was these?' the young bobby had asked, rather sharply, I thought, at the time, and followed it up with an even more stupid, 'Have you any idea where they've gone?'

I was about to give him an abrasive mouthful, but I held my tongue. The poor devil was maybe twenty-one, unused to tinkers as he was to life, and he was probably only trying to be helpful. Frankly, I felt more like bursting into tears than treating him to a blast of fiery eloquence. Eight months of my life had been literally thrown down the drain, eight months of psychology, sweat, toil and more psychol-

'I sat there in my untidy house upon my rocking chair . . .'

ogy. The young bobby snapped me out of my misery with a rather stupid, 'Cheer up, you've got some dogs left, anyway.'

It didn't help, and I was about to come out with something caustic when the phone went.

'Do you mate Jack Russells?' said a rather Birmingham-accented female.

'Not personally,' I snapped. 'You go to prison for it,' and slammed down the phone, but the young policeman had gone.

My gloom, normally only just below the surface anyway, plummetted my spirits to an all-time low.

Mo turned up on the Saturday to beg some sheep's heads for his dogs. 'You must have some,' he said rather spitefully. 'There's two dogs you won't be feeding.'

'I thought you said travellers didn't touch merle dogs,' I chided. 'Some expert, Mo.'

'No, not merle dogs,' he said. 'Wall-eyed dogs, moonpies.'

'You let me down there, Mo,' I said, partly because I felt he had, and partly in despair at my loss.

'Never understand you, Bri,' he said as he drove away, shaking his head.

45

Moses Aaron Smith

Alan phoned that night to tell me he had bought a litter of merle collie pups for me – at a next-to-nothing price, possibly because Alan, in an attempt to cheer me up, had subsidized my purchase. It helped, I suppose, but not a lot. It still left me at least two years behind in my project, for I'd have to rear the puppies to fifteen months, mate the bitch to a greyhound and wait another four months to have a puppy to train. The offer was kind and I took it, but the thought of going through the palaver of rearing, breeding and training daunted me a bit. Still, Alan brought up the litter, and I began to train a bright, merle-coloured bitch. It wasn't the same, and much as I tried, I just couldn't put my heart into it as wholeheartedly as when I had trained Merle. She was a cute puppy, very bright, attractive and easy to teach, but she simply wasn't Merle.

Fathom came out of dock, and I began training her in earnest, and perhaps the reason why she is such an incredible hunter today is quite simply because I put such gargantuan efforts into training her, simply to forget the loss of Merle. Personally, I think it is impossible to train more than one lurcher at a time anyway, and if Merle had been around, I'm sure Fathom would be only a canny little hunter, not the first-class hunting-up, bird-catching lurcher which she is today. But I never quite attained the link with her that I had with Merle. Fathom was faster, quicker off the mark, had just as good a nose, and was a useful bird dog, but the link between us was missing somehow.

With a hint of irony, maybe a note of despair, I began work on the book I was to entitle *The Complete Lurcher*, cribbing huge pieces of my diary of the early training of Merle to make up the book. I felt a fraud, writing about how tractable he was, knowing that he could well be dead in some canal with a block of concrete round his neck. Somehow the news of my writing the book got around, and that evening a man claiming to be a British Field Sports Society official (but then, who isn't a BFSS official these days?) phoned, angrily suggesting, nay demanding, that I withdraw the book *Rogues and Running Dogs* as it concerned poaching. I was too staggered to reply, but that evening I rewrote the plan of *The Complete Lurcher* to include a massive chapter on poaching – which in any case is the rightful work of a true lurcher, despite what legitimate coursers state.

Christmas came and went, uncelebrated, unwanted, and my only Christmas thoughts were that the shops would be shut for four days, thereby inconveniencing me a hell of a lot. My friend Joey Carey arrived on Boxing Day, looking a bit sheepish about a cake his wife had made me.

'The old battleaxe' – he is one of the five happily married men I know – 'says you look half-starved, Bri – best have this,' he said, throwing the cake on the table with an embarrassed look on his face. 'Seed your merle lurcher in Nuneaton.' My ears pricked. 'Least, I thought it were 'im.' My spirits dropped. 'He were running like hell towards the A5 – could 'ave been a collie I suppose, though,' he said, sleeving his mouth. 'Tried to stop to pick 'im up but he ran like hell across the fields. Like as if I'd kicked the bugger. Suppose it could 'ave been a collie, though,' he said, trying not to raise my hopes again.

'Personally my money is that he'd be in the bottom of a pool somewhere,' I said.

'Yeh, I suppose you could be right. Funny sort of dog,' he said. 'Don't see why you liked him – he were an ugly bugger' (the past tense came all too easily to everyone). 'You know, it could 'ave been 'im running,' he said passively. 'Looked exactly like him, nervy, shy, dead ugly. White face.' My hopes soared. 'Probably a collie, though,' he added. 'Seen a lot of collies his colour – an ugly colour,' he threw in for good measure, and left, leaving me wondering if he could indeed have seen Merle.

My advertisement for 'Dog lost. Reward offered' went into the papers with a description that made it clear that the dog was no Adonis so the reward wouldn't be high, and I began to get some response mostly of a curious nature. A chap from Daventry phoned to sympathize and offered me a large male chow full pedigree, but funny with children (shucks, so am I, so I could have used this dog perhaps). A quaint old lady from Middleton phoned to say she'd found Merle. I raced over in Henry's car only to find a pied mongrel greyhound, every bit as much a lurcher as Merle perhaps, but not quite what I wanted. We left after promising to find the dog a home, and Chris Turner, an accountant friend, has him now. When I arrived home shortly after ten, my phone was ringing. A chap from Wednesbury had not found Merle exactly, but he had a little of saluki whippet collie or something or other that might be exactly what I wanted. They weren't, but I thanked him and put the phone down. I needed these well wishers like I needed a hole in the head, but I suppose everybody was trying to help, and quite a few phoned merely to offer sympathy.

A month went by, and another followed, and I gave up all thought of recovering Merle and got on with the intensive training session with Fathom. She came on in leaps and bounds, improving a hundredfold by dint of my new interest in her. Watching Fathom improve so dramatically, I almost began to forget the hurt at losing Merle.

I lay in bed one night, troubled by my inadequacy as a teacher and listening to the dogs' erratic barking. It's peculiar, but whenever I am upset by anything the dogs are also unquiet and my nights will be spent smacking the tops of the kennels to silence them. That particular night was purgatory, and five times I ran out to smack the tops of the kennels to stop the almost insane barking. Funnily enough, Vampire, who is normally fairly silent, was raising absolute hell in the run, screaming and leaping at his kennel door. It could only be a fox, I thought, so I harnessed up my beam and went out to settle the matter. At the door of the run I flicked on the beam and the shock nearly bowled me over. At the end of the run, pawing his kennel to open it, was Merle, exhausted, his feet bleeding, his coat stained with diesel oil.

He swayed slightly as I ran towards him and made as if to run away. Twice he toppled and ran, but the third time he simply crumpled and lay there, too weak to move. I ran forward and shone the beam on him examining his wounds, his bruises, his torn and bleeding feet by torchlight. Two ribs were broken and an ugly rip had been torn in his scalp. He looked ghastly, like an RSPCA appeal poster, and twice I checked his markings to be absolutely certain it was the right dog. I reached down to carry him into the house. It was an easy job. He weighed less than twenty-three pounds!

6 *Recovery and the Sweet Scent of Diesel*

Merle was back. That was the main thing. And though he had probably been subjected to all the infections flesh is heir to, a week or so in isolation for an inoculated dog – a dog vaccinated against distemper, hard pad, hepatitis and leptospirosis – will usually be enough to show up whatever new bugs he has brought on to the premises. And isolation it had to be, for terriers are fairly quick to detect a weak member of a pack and to gang up on and sort out the said member. In fact, quite a few mammals actively encourage the weak of their species to expire. Man alone, I suppose, looks after his sick, his weak, his senile – and come to think of it, man doesn't make all that good a job of it either.

I isolated Merle, put him in a shed away from the rest, gave him a shot of multi-purpose long-range antibiotic – a universal specific of the sort vets give when they haven't a clue to the nature of a dog's illness. Merle was emaciated, his skin simply stretched over the ribs like a bender tent canvas, his hide dappled with oil and mange. Basically, his pitiful state was the result of a combination of factors. First, as soon as his captors had recognized that he was no hare dog – they probably reckoned it had been a mistake to steal him – food would have been in short supply for him, and he would have been fed only when there was a superabundance of flesh, and then given the least edible viands available. Secondly, Merle was reluctant to take food from anyone else. He even refused food from Terry, and Merle knew Terry very well. The icy weather hadn't helped him, that was for sure, for most of his days 'out' had experienced below-zero temperatures. Nor had the distance he had run to make it home helped his constitution. He had probably scavenged, or perhaps made an occasional kill, but it seemed unlikely that he could have lived by hunting like a Walt Disney runaway, and he certainly had not gone and befriended an old man or dying child like some tear-jerking Bank Holiday movie critter.

'Sweet Jesus,' Alex Turner said, gazing at the wound on Merle's head – a wound turning necrotic around the edges and beginning to smell badly. 'I bet you could tell a tale if you could talk. What sort of lunatic would gash a dog like this?' he said menacingly.

Merle

I shook my head. Merle could have told a tale right enough, a tale strange enough to put Lassie's to shame, enough to make the Greyfriars Bobby story look like Little Lord Fauntleroy's, but I doubt if the gash in his head had been put there by tinkers. Many do neglect their dogs, as a glance at any mud-splattered tyre-littered site will show, but I've yet to meet one who sets out to be deliberately cruel to a dog. Tinkers are usually uncaring rather than cruel. The chances were that he picked up the rip stealing from a bin belonging to an over-zealous house dweller, or maybe quite simply as a result of a road accident. The mange, the diesel-oil burns, that curiously eventually grow out as brown patches on the blue merle, were mute testimony to the place he had lived in with the people who had taken him, for most tinkers and their dogs have traces of oil on them. My bet would be that at their first attempt to try 'der little dog', Merle had bolted and started for home.

An emaciated dog whose condition is due to some disease such as distemper or leptospirosis – particularly leptospirosis – takes ages to recover and fleshes out very slowly. A healthy, skeleton-thin dog, and Merle, at twenty-three pounds, was skeleton thin, recovers very rapidly, particularly if his condition is due only to malnutrition and sundry neglect. The normal veterinary practice is to give good food, cooked meats, eggs and so on, gradually lest the stomach should be shocked by a sudden adequate or more than adequate diet. My own particular veterinary treatment is a bit more primitive and a heck of a sight more basic. I simply buy an overfat dead battery hen and throw the entire carcass to the underweight dog. Quite a few 'how to look after your dog' book writers would throw up their hands in horror at such a diet, stating that it causes punctured bowels, binding and death. But I've never found any harm feeding such a diet, and I've experienced nothing but success in feeding damaged, emaciated, lacerated and mauled dogs this diet of fat hens. True, it could cause some discomfort in a papillon or death maybe in a chihuahua, but little harm comes from feeding such food to a strong, robust dog like a lurcher, a dog as yet unspoilt by the show craze which allows weak and sickly canine specimens to perpetuate their ailment-ridden blood lines simply because they have such and such a show point. I've never encountered a punctured gut in my dogs – and I have all my fatal casualties autopsied. Enough of diet, however. Sufficient to say that Merle recovered quickly from his state of emaciation, and although his wounds took some little time to heal, he fleshed out rapidly.

But while his physical wounds knit rapidly, his mental hurt took longer to heal. He had been suspicious of strangers before, avoiding the hand that reached out to pat him, skulking out of reach when an unfamiliar voice called him. Now he became almost paranoid about familiarity of this nature and refused to let anyone, apart from myself, put a lead around his neck. Anyone who tried to take him on a lead would find they had a barking, rearing neurotic on the end of the tether. Yet his relationship with me became, if anything, even more tightly knit, and there seemed to be no limit to the tasks he would let me teach him.

You know, I really do jump the gun sometimes. When all is said and done, when every shred of evidence is examined, there is no real proof that he was stolen by those tinkers, and only a series of remarkable coincidences tends to give me reason to believe he was. True, the tinkers had watched me race to Merle's pen and the two most valued dogs disappeared next day. True, Merle returned covered in diesel oil and grease, but he could have acquired those stains during his attempt to find his way home, maybe acquired them by sleeping under lorries in scrap yards and such places. Remarkable coincidences perhaps, but still scarcely enough to be able to prove beyond reasonable doubt, as the law says, that so and so actually stole him, and certainly not enough to get a conviction in any court of law. A few weeks after his return, however, an incident occurred which, while not actually proof, convinced me as to who had actually perpetrated his theft.

Some tinkers turned up on my doorstep – as I've said, I live in a tinker corridor, a route used by every travelling man, good and bad alike, in the Midlands. Most cause no harm and only come this way because of the water taps under the near-by canal bridge – taps that provided water for canal people, water gipsies, at one time as itinerant as the tinkers who now use the taps. Most itinerants try their luck at the 'Have you any scrap iron, antiques?' routine (unlikely in my case, the antiques, I mean), or quite simply, 'Do you want any cut-price tarmacing doing on your place, sir?' Well, one day my peace and quiet was disturbed by a knock on the door, and glancing through the window I saw a pair of travellers get out of their brand-new Volvo and amble to my door to join the third.

I glanced down at Merle, and every hair on his body was standing on end, his muscles quivering with fear. He had never liked strangers, never gone out of his way to be sociable with them, unlike Fathom, who actually had to be restrained from getting into visitors' parked cars, but Merle had never displayed such antipathy to people before or since. I opened the door and he shot under the phone table, baring his lips at the tinkers and giving them a low menacing growl as they began their requests for tarmacing jobs. I was fascinated, and later that week when another tinker called about buying 'de leetle dog in der run' (Fathom), I subjected Merle to contact with the man – a man in working clothes, a far cry from the Volvo driver and his mates. But the reaction was the same – a rasping snarl, hackles raised and every inch of the dog displaying marked antipathy to the traveller.

I spoke to Moses about it, telling him the tale from start to finish. He listened patiently until the end and said, quite simply, 'Diesel oil'. Then he elaborated after he saw my puzzled face, 'Most travellers smell of diesel oil, for even the ones with Volvos don't get much of a chance to bath all that regularly and you can pick up a sniff or so of this oil even when you pass 'em in the street. To a dog it must appear a thousand times stronger.'

Merle had not, like James Arigho in Vesey-FitzGerald's book, been able to spot a pure-bred tinker on sight, but his scent of diesel oil obviously brought back curious and unpleasant memories. Funnily enough, although he got over the hang-ups acquired during his six weeks of captivity, he never went near a tinker again.

7 'My Sort of Dog, Jimmy'

Throughout his entire life, Merle's shape and conformation has only had one admirer, one person who immediately recognized him as a lurcher, one person who admired his type, shape and weight. I'd have been happier if he hadn't, for I knew what the admirer had in mind for Merle. Come to think of it, I'd have been happier if the admirer hadn't been Jodie Faws.

I'd met Jodie ten years before, and the real problem with writing a book like this is that I realize how quickly time passes and how damned old I'm getting. I was broke at the time, if I remember, so times haven't changed all that much, and I was the owner of a big, fawn, rough-coated bitch, a none-too-clever blend of deerhound, greyhound, saluki with an infinitesimally small dash of collie blood to ameliorate the idiot mix. With Bear, the result of such a cocktail, the colllie blood hadn't helped much, for whereas there must have been more stupid and intractable dogs than Bear, all I can say is that (salukis excepted) I've never owned or seen one. If all one required was a quick slip at a hare, a lightning-quick run up, an almost equally lightning snatch at the prey and a mindless couldn't care less amble back, Bear was ideal. Ask her to hunt up, to work out a situation, to be obedient, to react to a command quickly or even get out of the way of oncoming traffic, and it would be a different matter. She was short in brain, I admit, but very high on speed and courage, and she'd nail foxes, pin badgers (I lost a litter when a very pregnant Bear exercizing at night slammed straight into a badger), and she was fairly good at bigger stuff as well (but considering a recent court case concerning the 'bigger stuff', I would just as soon pass over that subject). All in all, Bear was a moderately good, somewhat moronic, rough-coated, saluki-eared, coursing greyhound, not a lurcher, and there is not much more to be said about Bear.

When she came in season I decided to breed from her, not as many lurcher breeders would have you believe to improve the quality of stock within the breed, but simply because I was on my backside for money and there is usually a good market for big, powerful, rough-coated 'far-away looking' lurchers. I mated her to a half-bred deerhound, a genuine half-bred, not the type usually advertised as deerhound/greyhound – a hotchpotch of breeds that levels out as anything between 18 and 32 inches – but a genuine one, the result of mating a rather sinister, mean old Ardkinglas deerhound, passed on several times with pedigree free to a good but country home simply because of his interest in sheep, cats, dogs and anything that moved. Once, during a walk in a fashionable shopping centre of an even more fashionable high street, this dog had seen a Siamese cat sitting atop a Mary Quant pile of garments, and the next moment pop-art cat and deerhound with a liberal sprinkling of glass were strewn around the shop. The same day, he lifted a Doberman pinscher, no mean feat, shook it hard and flung it down, its neck at a ridiculous angle. He was a canine liability, in fact, but when he was mated to a first-class coursing greyhound his pups sold for £30 a piece (and this was sixteen years ago, when £30 was more than I earned in a week – come to think of it, I don't earn much more now). One of those pups, a steel-grey monster with mean piggy eyes, a 28-inch shoulder, a bad reputation for livestock killing and a rat-trap mouth, was mated to Bear.

She whelped six puppies, all steel grey, all rough coated – five neat, greyhoundy, stylish whelps, one of which won at Lambourn. The sixth puppy was Mac. Mixing bloodlines to breed lurchers is a risky business, as the chromosomes, genes and whatever else constitutes the machinery of genetics usually function totally independently of the breeder's wishes. I've seen nearly pure deerhounds, 30-inch, elegant, rough-coated dogs, collies not out of place in a sheep-dog trial and a beast resembling a Bedlington terrier and a Welshhound thrown from a litter of puppies supposedly bred from two deerhound/greyhound parents (genuine – always genuine), while the number of dogs produced in most lurcher litters that could be run on a greyhound flapping track is staggering. Still, my litter was nothing to boast about, though Mac certainly was special.

Way back in the ancestry of any greyhound is a dash of bulldog blood – bulldogs damned near the size of bull mastiffs mixed in with the native greyhound blood to give 'poke' and fury to take on anything. Deerhounds likewise have a line or so dating back to giant Celtic hounds – dogs whose dimensions matched a skull dug from the Irish peat bogs half a century ago, a dog which would have (according to Carson Richie) been 48 inches at the shoulder – a colossal animal. Somehow, the genes of this long-gone giant, the genes of the old mastiff type of bulldog and a few stray genes of another monstrosity had got together and produced Mac. The mix was then stirred, shaken and laughed over by some divine genetic prankster.

At eight weeks old he stood a full head above the rest of the litter and was seven pounds heavier. In spite of the rough coat, which can conceal a multitude of sins, as any lurcher judge will testify, his legs were obviously heavy boned – so heavy, in fact, that they would not have appeared out of place on a mastiff. His head was broad – not the elegant head of the deerhound nor the long brainless cranium of a greyhound, but an enormous flat, broad head of a pit bull terrier. He was also aggressive, even as a babe, hogging the food dish, menacing the others, threatening anything that came near his meat, and once putting a set of needle-sharp teeth in my hand when I tried to move him away from his evening meal to allow his litter mates a chance. He was an amazing-looking dog, I thought at the time, but he was also unsaleable – or so I thought.

My advertisement in *Exchange and Mart* looked very unprepopessing: 'Lurchers. Deerhound and Greyhound genuine [well, it's a force of habit, isn't it?]. Dam a very fast lurcher bitch £15,' carefully omitting Bear's total lack of brain, her completely untrainable nature and the savage disposition of the sire, vowing I'd settle for £10 if someone haggled, and throw in Mac free of charge to anyone who was a bit in doubt, the 'Well, I'll call back later' type. Funnily enough, you can tell a lot about the life a puppy will lead by the questions people ask about it. Will it definitely be rough coated? (I want this dog as an image maker.) What height will it make? Are both mother and father on view? (I've been told nothing above 23 inches is any good.) Are you sure of its breeding? (I've been sent to the cleaners before.) Will it take every hare it sees? (I am an idiot.)

I steeled myself to deal with the callers.

Thursday morning, shops open, *Exchange and Mart* on sale. Thursday evening, first buyer.

'Is this the only litter you have, Jimmy?' said a broad Glaswegian accent, accentuated until it resembled a composite of all the characters on the Moira Anderson Hogmanay show. 'Is it, Jimmy?' he asked somewhat impetuously, without having even seen the litter.

The would-be buyer was perhaps my age, with dark, slicked-back hair and rather shifty eyes, eyes that took in the whole place at a glance, casing the joint, as they say in underworld slang. I felt almost ashamed that I wasn't one of those dog dealers who could field sixty assorted puppies, all from the best lurchers in Britain, all properly pedigreed deerhound and greyhound, of course, and all for sale!

'These the parents – Jimmy?' he said, nodding at the sire and the dam in the next pen, the sire sulking morosely, the dam frantically trying to lick him through the wires (in addition to being stupid, Bear was anybody's).

I nodded.

'Are they stock worriers, Jimmy?'

A curious question, so, with a hint of embarrassment, I explained I'd borrowed the dog for the duration of the advertisement and that he wasn't all that good with stock (he was a sod, actually, having killed cats, dogs, sheep and poultry).

'Is the bitch intelligent' – I waited for it – 'Jimmy?'

'Not really,' I admitted rather sheepishly, for I'm not very good at selling, but at least I'm honest.

'Retrieve, will she?'

'Not very well,' I confessed. 'She's got saluki blood, I'm afraid' (which sure doesn't help the trainability of the dog).

'Hm,' he replied, and for good measure, 'Jimmy.'

Well, I'd lost a sale, but there'd be more. I was sure of that, for at that time there was a ready market for lurchers, and I was about to say 'Sorry, but that's all we have,' and go indoors and try to earn an honest quid by translating some book of spells written in a mixture of Latin and bastard Hebrew (as I've said, it takes all sorts) when he continued, 'All for sale, is it?'

I nodded again.

'Bad with stock, are they?'

I almost hung my head in shame.

'I'll take the big one,' he muttered, peeling off £15 and nodding at Mac.

I couldn't believe my luck. First buyers usually pick up the best puppies, and here was buyer No. 1 walking off with Mac the giant, the ugliest pup I'd ever bred – and I've bred some ugly ones – when he had the choice of the lot.

'If it's no good, bring it back, and I'll refund your money,' I offered as a let-out clause, a dangerous let-out clause, as lurcher folk change dogs with their fancies. 'I'll just take your name,' I added, getting out my diary.

'Faws,' he replied. 'Jodie Faws.'

Faws – a name steeped in strange, curious antiquity, a name equated with rascally behaviour, villainy and outlaw clans along the Scottish borders. I stopped writing.

'Are you a gipsy?'

He nearly hit the roof. 'I'm bloody not, Jimmy, what the hell do you mean?'

I had visions of Mac going back in the pens and money back in his pocket. 'Faws is a famous gipsy name,' I tried, though 'notorious' would be a better word, though best not described that way under the circumstances.

'Well, I'm bloody not a gyppo,' he snorted, upset, perhaps, because few people resembled the typical man-in-the-street idea of a Romany as much as Jodie Faws. 'I'm not a bloody gyppo, Jimmy,' he repeated as if challening me.

'I've written and researched the Faws,' I offered, convinced that any moment now he would launch himself at me, lashing at me with a chunk of iron with real old, traditional Romany violence.

'Not my bloody family, Jimmy, not mine,' he almost shouted.

It was not a particularly good start to a relationship, I admit, but I somehow managed to stay away from the subject of Romanies and after a while we became fairly regular associates, though not (Jimmy) firm friends, I must add.

I like Scotland. It is a country of extremes, producing its share, no more than its share, of really wild eccentrics – eccentrics that put me in the shade. When the land produces intellectuals, they dwarf other intellectuals; when Scotland produces tycoons, they turn out to be billionaires like Carnegie, able to buy if not influence friends; and as for outlaws, bandits, brigands, well, Robin Hood wouldn't have stood a chance. Compared to his Scottish counterparts, Robin's merry men resembled a meeting of the Sherwood Forest Gay Club. Take, for instance, Sawney Bean, executed, so one legend says, in 1405, together with his family, who not ony robbed most of the population of Galloway but, in true thrifty Scottish manner, ate them as well. But a century later, the Faws or Faas – take your choice, it's the same name – appeared in Scotland and turned the country inside out.

Now, as conmen go, the Faas, Faws, Fors or any other variants were just about the tops. They were gipsies, descendants of a ragged band that strolled into Paris in 1427 on the feast of St John the Beheaded (John the Baptist), described by a chronicle as the poorest and ugliest people in the world. The former status was soon to be rectified, however, for by 1527 the Faws were firmly entrenched in the court of James V of Scotland, a gullible sort of chap who honestly believed that John Faw, ragged and of no fixed abode, was really the Earl of Egypt, dispossessed of his land and titles by the wicked Turks. James V gave them shelter, lands and goods, but before long the king began to realize that if the Turks had thrown the Faws out of Egypt, then the Turks had had a damn good reason, for the Faws became what is known in Walsall criminal parlance as 'A' stealers, people who only steal things beginning with an A – a coach, a horse, a sheep, etc. Before long James began to regret making these 'Egyptians' welcome. In 1530, the courts were so fed up with the taking ways of this family that they had a quick whip round and raised enough money to send the whole damned lot of Faws, Faas, Fors to Norway.

But, as they say, you can't keep a good Faws down, and a hundred years later we find the Faws living Carver Doone type of outlaw lives, fighting a hill-billy battle with the Jeffersons in Rothbury Forest around Bedlington. Verily, the sundry permutations of the house of Faws, Faas, Fors were not a people to trifle with – to hang, to lynch to burn maybe, and many suffered these fates, but to trifle with, never. In 1779, one of the clan in Durham ate a live cat for a bet, a fairly popular activity at fairs at that time, but I digress.

I lost track of Jodie for about two years after this, until one day his untaxed Bedford 30-hundredweight ('Goes well without tax, Jimmy') pulled up outside my place and disgorged Jodie and two really villainous-looking chaps with hand-scarred faces and the look of Barbary pirates out for the night in Scunthorpe. With them leaped Mac – Jodie's name, not mine – now aged two and a half. He had been an unlovely puppy, but he had mellowed with age, matured, perhaps, and grown into a hideous adult. Mac had levelled out at 32 inches of heavy muscle and bone, a hybrid 'twixt a bull terrier and an Irish wolfhound with just a soupçon of something unpleasant stirred in for good measure.

'What d'ye think of him, Jimmy? – For Christ's sake, don't touch him, Jimmy,' he shouted. 'He'll take your hand off – the bastard,' he added, gleefully glowing with pride at the raging monster he was holding back with both hands on its choker. 'Just try to get in the van, Jimmy, just try.'

'No thanks,' I whispered, my voice dying in my throat at the idea of the brute attacking me, feeling just a bit like Dr Frankenstein when he realized his monstrous creation had run amok.

'See you, Jimmy,' Jodie shouted driving off, Mac snarling at me through the window, the epitome of a Baskerville remover.

After that, Faws – 'Call me Jodie, Jimmy, call me Jodie' – came maybe once a year, always with men of such a savage nature that even Ron, a Borstal-trained plasterer and expert in the head butt, the knee to the groin and himself a general GBH merchant, said, 'Jesus, where is he getting them from? They're a ferocious-looking bunch'; and for Ron to say that was going some.

I missed Jodie's visits for about two years, though it would be tactless to ask Jodie or someone of his ilk why he'd not been around or how he had spent the missing time. But shortly after Merle's terrific mauling from Vampire, when Merle was still recuperating from a dozen deep punctures and a score more of punishing bruises, favouring one leg and generally looking out of sorts, Jodie arrived as usual in his untaxed, rusty Beford van, the seats of which had been torn to pieces by the now very ageing Mac, whose looks and temper were not improved by senility. Also, during some adventure or other, God knows what, Mac had lost an ear, and a huge partly healed though unstitched wound stretched between his mouth and the place where the ear should have been. I gazed in wonder at the monster, his torn face, his lifted lip, and the ominous roar seeking to come through from his clenched teeth.

'Serve me well he has, Jimmy. Come for another. I've never told anyone where I bought this one, Jimmy, don't want too many of the buggers all over the countryside. Unique he is.'

I agreed. I was also glad he'd shut up about where he'd bought the animal.

'Come for another one,' he repeated. 'Mac's just about past it,' and then added ominously, 'Not strong enough any more to pull 'em down.'

What in hell has he been catching? Mac was obviously capable of pulling down a dinosaur or a mammoth. I invited Jodie in, together with his friend.

Owen, a schoolboy in my class, nudged me. 'Sir, look at him, look at Jodie's mate.'

'Yes, he's pretty odd,' I admitted under my breath, looking at the pockmarked face, the lank hair, the earrings and the inevitable eagle giving a serpent a hell of a bad time tattooed up his arm.

'Sir,' Owen persisted, 'look at his hands.'

He had the inevitable 'love' and 'hate' tatooed on the knuckles, but something was wrong. 'LOVE' has four letters, 'HATE' another four, yet there was one finger spare, one finger on each hand unmarked except for a crown or club or similar device. Strange, 'love' was spelt correctly, so was 'hate'.

'Jesus,' I hissed aloud, 'he's got six fingers,' but thank God neither hard-case heard me as they were fondling Merle.

'Selling him?'

I shook my head.

'Pity,' Jodie replied.

'Yer,' chimed in the many-fingered friend, who spoke by shooting words off the palate and down his nose, 'Yer.'

'Pity,' repeated Jody. 'He's my sort of dog.'

At last success, someone who likes Merle, someone who didn't ridicule his shape.

'Collie/greyhound?' hissed Jodie.

I was jubilant. Jodie was the first and only person to recognize Merle as some sort of lurcher and not simply a collie or a crossbred.

'Yer,' spat out the six-fingered one with a snort.

'Ye need a drop of collie blood', Jodie went on, still gazing at the injured Merle, fingering his ears. 'Ye would na sell him, Jimmy?' he repeated.

'Yer,' said the multi-digital one, his eyes taking on almost an intelligent look.

'Aye,' Jodie went on. 'Ye need collie blood in a lurcher, particularly for our work. Innit, Welshy?' he boomed at the curious-looking associate who seemed deaf as well as unusually shaped. 'Could live off a dog like this, Welshy,' he shouted, and received the inevitable answer.

I swelled with pride – a fellow collie/greyhound addict, a member of a family who had actually lived off hunting, poaching, etc.., and who appreciated my dog, but that 'etc.' part had yet to be explained.

'Got another one of the same breed collie/greyhound like, Jimmy?'

I shook my head and explained the Dai Fish story and the coming of Merle. I also explained collie intelligence, collie sagacity.

'And the herding instinct is important, innit, Welshy?' put in Jodie.

'Yer,' Welshy replied, snapping out of picking his teeth with a strip torn off a Pepsi tin.

'If ye get one of same breed, Jimmy, no colour, no matter, where he be a black or one o' they, Jimmy, let me know. That dog's mine, Jimmy. Soon as ye get one, I'll buy him, I'll buy him unseen. It's a brae cross, Jimmy, exactly what I need. Could live offen one of them as easy as wink.'

I was feeling quite proud by the time Jodie and Welshy were ready to leave.

'He's been a loyal dog, has Mac,' Jodie said, shaking his head and reaching forward to stroke the monster. 'Loyal.'

Mac roared and struck at the hand, which was withdrawn as quickly as a conjurer taking a rabbit out of a hat.

'Loyal,' Jodie repeated, examining his grazed knuckles. 'I've lived off this damn dog, Jimmy, lived offen him,' Jodie repeated, tears of nostalgia in his eyes.

'Yer,' confirmed Welshy.

'Done everything I asked of him. Loyal, Jimmy'.

I agreed with them as it seemed best to agree at the time.

Merle had ambled to the doorway and stood there, bandaged and looking quite ill.

'If ye change ye mind, Jimmy, and want to sell me the dog, it's me for him. He'll do my job a treat. A brae dog, a dog and a half.'

He opened the back door of the untaxed van and the stench hit me, and I realized at once why Merle would suit him, why a dog with collie blood would do 'his sort of job'. Piled high to the top of the van, making the sides of the Bedford bulge, their throats cut, their fur torn through dog bites, were sheep. Clearly, herding instinct was important to Jodie, and clearly a collie-bred dog would be priceless.

He waved good-bye. 'Nice to see yer again, Jimmy, innit, Welshy?'

'Yer'; and they drove off into the evening.

8 Ephraim Pride

Winter slipped and slithered to Christmas. I arrived home to find a shaggy lurcher in my kennels and Ephraim sitting on his haunches in my porch. It was to be expected. Travellers are rarely in possession of calendars, and few know the date, but regular as clockwork they turn up at summer solstice fairs as though motivated by some biological body clock. Come the week before Appleby, and the roads are full of travellers all moving towards the fells like a caribou migration. Likewise, as winter comes, so Ephraim arrives in my village, parking his horse-drawn pot cart near the most bleak of the fields towards Catton. He has done so since before I drifted into this district, and no doubt will do so long after I have gone. Ephraim's bachelor life seems to change little from year to year, and he seems to age far more slowly than ordinary folk. Each year the first leaf fall finds him sitting in my porch with curios for sale or as gifts.

He is a forbidding-looking character. A great many middle-aged Romanies look very ferocious, as wild and intractable as John the Baptist, with long black hair, gold earrings and heavy sovereign rings on the fingers, but Ephraim's gold teeth – each and every tooth in his head is gold capped – are his most peculiar features. 'Didikai,' said Mo disparagingly as usual, for anyone who owns a mobile ice-cream cart and is not immediately recognizable as a Romany is in danger of being dubbed didikai by Mo. 'With a name like Ephraim, he's got to be a didi.' It seemed a curious comment coming from a man with a name like Moses Aaron Smith. 'Wumper,' he added, meaning one who dries his washing on a hedge rather than on a washing line – a curious type of class distinction, I've always thought. 'Ask 'im about his teeth,' he suggested. 'That's the only way didikais keep their friends from stealing their money, keeping it in their bleeding teeth.'

This strange statement may have a ring of truth about it, for ten years ago after Stowe Fair, a didikai was held down by thugs – not travellers, I must add – and had his gold teeth ripped out with pliers. It would be a brave man who attempted to divest Ephraim of his wealth, however, for Ephraim is above six feet in height and the long bluish scar that splits his brown, almost Arab-like face gives him a ferocious appearance. His pedigree is also formidable, for his father

'parking his horse-drawn pot-cart'

was a direct descendant of the gaudily dressed prize fighter, Posh Price (Posh meaning 'proud', not 'half' as it does in Romany), a bare-knuckle pugilist of some note.

Ephraim is a man I trust, however. I don't feel that way about many of the travellers who pass through this village, I must admit, but I have never known Ephraim to be dishonest. Truth to tell, on the other hand, his father was the greatest exponent of the violin trick. Let me explain. Some years ago, and Ephraim must be past sixty, I suppose, Ephraim's father met up with a thoroughly disreputable character called Captain Foster, a graduate of Eton, Cambridge and Parkhurst, IOW, who had decided criminal tendencies and was a top-rate con man. The 'rike', as they say in thieves' cant, was this. Ephraim's father, who, looking like a Hungarian gipsy (he certainly had Kalderashi blood), would go into a pub with an old violin under his arm, ask the landlord to keep it for him and put it up along the optics as a sort of display item. The old man would stress that the violin had sentimental value and that there was local hostility to gipsies. Exit Ephraim's dad. Two days later, in would stroll Captain Foster, garishly and expensively dressed, and order a gin and 'it' or whatever else cashiered officers normally drank. After sipping his drink, he'd ask to see the violin up there with the optics.

'My God, a Stradivarius,' he'd almost scream. 'A Stradivarius. I must have it. I'll give you a thousand pounds for it.' Enter wad of money big enough to choke a donkey.

'It's not mine to sell,' says the landlord rather sadly, but, scenting a fast buck, he'd add, 'I'll try and buy it, however.'

Exit Foster, promising to return next week to claim his music treasure. Two days later, enter Ephraim's dad to reclaim his violin. 'Would you care to sell it?' says the landlord, brandishing £20.

'It's an heirloom, all the way from Cremona' (the birthplace of Stradivarius), Old Pride adds for good measure.

Landlord promptly ups the price to £100, but Pride's father refuses to sell, even though he admits that he is desperate for money, for his wife and children are in need of expensive medical treatment. Landlord, being a 'good sort', usually ups the offer to £150, and Ephraim's dad tearfully hands over his most treasured possession, pocketing £150. Exit dad, like Captain Foster never to be seen again, leaving landlord the proud owner of a ten-bob violin. There are some funny people in this world, believe me, and a full eighty per cent of the population, myself included, are category A suckers, just pleading to be milked. All in all, the Prides are a subtle, injudicious blend of tinkers, *didikais*, show people, liberally dusted with an even more liberal dose of thieves and highwaymen (Jacob Pride was hanged for being a gentleman of the road), which was probably why Ephraim, who was a very reasonable sort of chap, decided to leave the tribe and go it alone in his pot cart. Pot cart – another term which I'd best explain.

Caravans or horse-drawn vardos are not the traditional Romany sort of dwelling. In fact, traditional seems hardly the word, for the first vardo appeared on the roads of Britain only 150 years ago, some people say as late as 1869. In fact, most other people, such as travelling showmen and quack medicine sellers (like those in an Italian spaghetti Western), had been using vardos long before the gipsy folk decided they were a good idea. The most primitive type of caravan was the pot cart, quite simply a tent on wheels or covered wagon, but of even these the Romanies were suspicious. Most Romanies of the early nineteenth century lived in bender tents of canvas stretched over ash hoops, as some Scottish itinerants do to this day. In George Borrow's *Lavengro*, the author is told by Ursula Herne, a sinister gipsy woman much skilled in drabbing (poisoning), 'We are not over fond of gorgios, brother, and we hates basket makers and folks that live in caravans.' Another fallacy about to be exploded. Few Romanies or itinerants had the skill or means to make their own vardos, in spite of what romantic tales of the road tell, but simply bought their elaborate patterned and carved vardos and wagons from firms in reading or Burton-on-Trent. In fact, the Calladines, called the Flash Calladines on account of their immaculate appearance, always bought their caravans from Dunton's of Reading, paying extraordinarily high prices for their baroque, customized vardos.

One of Pride's ancestors did, as a matter of fact, put one over on the Duntons, referred to by Ephraim as Mr Dunkins. One of the Prides went into Dunton's yard to order a very elaborate custom-built Reading vardo, putting down a nominal sum of money to clinch the deal. He insisted that the customizing should be so outlandish that only the designer or a pop artist would call it beautiful. Thereafter, one of the Prides called at the yard every day to hurry the work along, yet when it was finished, the vardo was allowed to stand in the premises of 30 King's Road, Reading, unwanted, gathering dust and using up valuable space in the yard. A relative of the 'shyster' (running cant for 'swindler') now called in and offered a pitiful sum to take the wagon off the Duntons hands – an offer which Sam Dunton, an honest man, famed for his integrity but not his patience, probably took up to rid himself of the hideously garish vehicle. The Prides were certainly professional tricksters. Treat a gipsy with respect, stated Alfred Dunton, and there's no better person. But, as Mo said, the Prides were not gipsies.

'his tiny coloured mare and rough Bedlington-type lurcher . . .'

Nevertheless, as I've told you, I like Ephraim and find his solitary, couldn't-care-for-anyone bachelor existence endearing if hard. Summer and winter alike, he lived in his pot hut of canvas draped over his pathetic worldly goods. (Most gyps are fine-weather travellers, he would add. They'd hole up in a house or semi-enclosed yard in winter.) Then he had only his tiny coloured mare and rough Bedlington-type lurcher for comfort. He is, indeed, one of the few travellers I've met who could keep and train a dog for more than a few months, for most chop and change dogs at a hell of a rate.

'Brung yer these,' he said rather sheepishly, throwing down five rusting, antique-looking gin traps on the floor. 'Don't pay to use 'em these days,' he added, like a piece of paternal advice to an erring boy. Gin traps were made illegal in 1953 after rabbits became not worth catching because of myxomatosis. You used to be able to pick up hundreds of the traps, just checking around fields, but now they're getting rare. 'Most old things are getting rare,' he added nostalgically. Nothing new, nothing modern is esteemed by Ephraim. 'Yer know, though,' he went on, 'yer can buy gins in this country if you send for them from abroad. Suppose they're cruel here but not abroad,' he put in somewhat paradoxically, I thought, but I understood what he meant. He leaned back in my one comfortable chair and lapsed into a curious language, a mixture of running cant, the language of thieves and Liverpudlian costers, and Shelta, a language that was old before Patrick troubled Ireland with Christianity.

I learned Shelta, adulterated with various cants, from Ephraim ten winters ago when his mare went lame and he was quartered too long near Catton – too long for his own liking, that is, not for others, for he is little trouble in the district, and though he takes the occasional rabbit, he causes little harm. (Would to God our local tinkers were of the same inclination.) Shelta is a curious language, a secret language of the road, more difficult to learn than Romany and spoken by quiet, soft-spoken, glib, Celtic tongues. It is a language few people care to learn. Sampson, the greatest authority on the language of itinerants, who went to various Shelta-speaking pubs, once had to run for his life when a wild and woolly tinker realized that Sampson was recording his conversation in a notebook. It is the most difficult language that I have ever tried to learn, for its ancient Celtic roots have been twisted and amended to a secret code by reversing words. Mac, the Celtic word for son, hence McCloud, Macpherson, Macgregor, has been amended to 'kam', while *kushnor*, probably a hybrid word twist from *nacsunor* (soft) and *shoshoi* (Romany), means hare.

'Ask 'im how he got his scar,' Moses had asked, for Moses, ever ready for me to get a good story, probably knew how Ephraim had

Gin traps

acquired that frightful blue rip that had all but torn his face in two. One night, when he came visiting, I did pluck up courage to question him about his hideous disfigurement, and after much dodging and darting he finally came up with this tale. He had been in his early twenties perhaps – few travellers can tell you their age or birthdays exactly – and he had just about abandoned the tribe or clan that was ruled or rather terrorized by a chap called Fierce Pride or Mether Pride (*methor*, probably Celtic, meaning a devil or unquiet spirit). A chance meeting then brought a group together in a pub near Doncaster, and for a while all had been old times, sweetness and light. As the ale went down, however, the mood grew darker and the Prides took to playing cards. Ephraim lost, as expected, for Mether had a reputation for being able to make a deck of cards talk (fifty-two disciples of the devil, was what Rebecca Smith, a religious fanatic Romany, had called a deck of playing cards). When Ephraim had lost his wad, flushed with drink and made overbold by booze, he had asked for a double or nothing wager, but they had only laughed at him, knowing he had no more money to bet. Finally Mether had given him a chance at an outrageous wager: all Ephraim's losings against Ephraim's index finger. The beer being in, the sense was not, and once more Mether dealt another hand. The total silence in the room chilled Ephraim sober and he suddenly realized the enormity of the stake. As expected, he lost, and Mether claimed his fee while Ephraim, clawing, screaming and fighting, was dragged off to the toilets to ensure he did not welch on the deal. He had managed to kick himself free, but not before his face had received a terrific 'cush' or wipe with a knife blade, a wound that ensured he lay up for weeks to enable the hideous gash to heal. He had stayed clear of the Prides before that day, but now he was destined to live as a solitary, moving away from the usual tinker routes. And lo, once again have I lost my tale in yet another digression into the world of odd people.

Ephraim drank his tea in silence. 'See yer got a collie now. Why, Bri, yer going to breed 'em, or maybe rustle sheep?' he added.

I explained that Merle was a lurcher, but Ephraim would have none of it. 'No, lurchers is like greyhounds, sleek like a whippet shape, look at Flor, a right "be"' (an Irish term meaning something femininely comely). 'Lurcher, that's a lurcher. Yours is a collie.'

He was quite adamant and I'd have been a fool to argue, for to tell the truth Merle could easily have passed for a smoothish-coated collie dog of the sort hill farmers used along the borders of Cumberland, the sort used to round up aggressive hill-bred rams.

'Ner, yours is a collie,' he repeated. 'Ner a lurcher.'

I shrugged and was silent. 'How much the traps, Ephraim?' I

changed the subject. 'Bid me,' he said, knowing my inability to cope with bidding, a system of haggling that seems second nature to a traveller.

'Just name a price, Ephraim,' I said, a touch peevishly for I loathe the custom of bidding.

'Tell you what,' he said, pointing at a hideous off-colour print of a badger bought for me by a class on the day the band left school. 'Throw in all the traps for der picture.'

I spat hands and sealed the deal. 'Done yer there,' said Mo later. 'Told you he was a didi. They steal horses as well,' he threw in for good measure, but I was glad to be rid of the terrible print, terrible even by Fifth Year, sec. mod. tastes.

As a bachelor, I always feel somewhat embarrassed by not being able to offer people a meal when they come to my house, especially since, prompted by my shabby attire and bachelor scruffiness, people always offer me food when I go to their homes.

'Come on, Ephraim,' I beckoned. 'I'll buy you a meal at the local Chinese restaurant.'

'Never been in a restaurant,' he said, a rather worried expression crinkling his scar. 'Ner, I wouldn't like it, people would watch me eating.'

'They watch me sometimes,' I laughed, but it took me three hours to persuade him.

He looked incongruous, I must admit, but settled near us was a skinhead with National Front slogans tatooed on his neck, while opposite, in leather gear, was a punk rocker girl whose green head was alluringly topped by a vermilion-coloured cockscomb of hair. Even so, the diners in the restaurant stared hard at Ephraim.

A Chinese waiter approached, his inscrutable face not showing any flicker of interest in either of us. I place both our orders, for Ephraim was deeply self-conscious about his illiteracy, but when the waiter returned with chop and chips twice and a soupçon of inscrutability, he spat out, 'You a hutter?'

I stared back, baffled at the question.

'I think he means hunter,' Ephraim whispered.

I nodded. After all, some of my friends think I qualify as such, though judging by a recent attack by the British Field Sports Society, hunter may seem a bit of a questionable term. I nodded again.

'You have phloxes?'

'No,' I replied, 'I hate gardening and I can't get phloxes.'

'You get phloxes,' he repeated, sounding like an extra from a badly made Charlie Chan film or a failed Fu Manchu character.

'I don't grow flowers,' I repeated.

'He means foxes,' hissed Ephraim, now terribly embarrassed.

'Foxes,' I corrected him.

'Yes, phloxes,' the waiter replied, even chancing a smile.

'You want a pet cub?' I queried.

'Not clubs, phloxes,' he said, somewhat peevishly.

I continued to stare back at him.

'They eat them, you prat,' hissed Ephraim, almost angrily. 'He wants foxes to eat.' After a short discussion our waiter left, having offered me £8 for a skinned carcass. Then he brought our bill. 'Do you have those who swim in the water?' he asked, making a swimming motion with his hands, as if to explain to this idiot who professed to be a 'hutter'.

'No, I'm not a fisherman,' I answered, writing out my cheque.

'No, not flish. Those who swim in the water. Not flish.'

'The bugger means otters,' whispered Ephraim, but I waived our host aside, astounded at the amazingly omnivorous tastes of Orientals.

We left the restaurant and walked back the three wet and miserable miles to my cottage.

Three foxes taken near Ephraim's cart to prove my point

'Yer know,' Ephraim began, 'you could make a living selling foxes to them folks. A living,' he repeated, 'and the skins would be worth summat as well. Yer'd need a good dog, though,' he added wistfully, 'a game 'un.'

'I have one,' I replied quietly.

'Ner, that's a collie, not a long dog,' he replied impatiently. 'It's a collie. Yer'd need a lurcher. The blue bugger's a collie and he'll not catch yer a fox to save his spotty hide.'

Oh, Ephraim Pride, if only you'd known how wrong you would be, you would have stuck to trading painted hosses, coloured ponies and flat carts and never ventured into the world of dogs or offered an opinion of fox-catching. Before the year was through, you would eat your words, Ephraim Pride.

I told Mo of the incident at the Chinese restaurant and the offers for fox and other meat.

'Bet Pride weren't shocked,' he sneered. 'Didis will eat foxes – and otters –' he nearly spat out. 'In fact,' he added wistfully, 'bet a didi would eat a didi.'

9 Trouble with Fathom

If I lived in a vardo, bow-topped or Reading, travelling the country and putting twenty miles a day under the wheels, if I treated the country in cavalier fashion, acting like a somewhat irregular Robin Hood, stealing from rich and poor alike (and keeping it all), Fathom would be my ideal lurcher. As it is, I live in a remote – well, sometimes remote – country cottage which I leave to work from 9 a.m. to 4 p.m. every day, and having to face the consequences of Fathom's malpractices is a decided liability.

There are many faster dogs than Fathom. On her bad days, I am faster than Fathom, and most muscle-bound lurchers will beat her to a frazzle at hares. There are probably many better rabbiting dogs

'If I lived in a vardo, bow-topped or Reading . . .'

'Scarcely a day goes by without a rabbit stowed behind the boots in the porch'

'Woolly, her speckled merle son, is well on the way to being one'

'. . . turning his head lest he should see their inane feathery hysteria'

than Fathom, although, with tongue-in-cheek pride, I have to admit that there aren't that many, for scarcely a day goes by when she does not materialize with a rabbit purloined from a near-by farm and stow it behind the boots in the porch. No, it is not for these qualities that Fathom has become famous in the district, for Fathom is what is known in gipsy parlance as a *kannechor* – a chicken thief, a dog who seeks out, catches and brings home other people's poultry – and I emphasize other people's, for if she were simply a chicken worrier it would be an easy habit to break. To break a *kannechor* is a different matter.

Forget the image of the dog who walks into a poultry-dappled farmyard, dealing death and destruction to all its denizens, making the place a charnel house of blood, death and destruction. Such a dog is not a *kannechor*. Such a beast is an untrained nuisance, and to call such a creature *kannechor* would be like referring to Raffles as a sneak-thief. A *kannechor* is something different, for he is the cracksman among canine villains, the thief who runs riot in the countryside without getting caught, but a dog who looks every inch the fireside pet. Fathom is just such a beast, which is not surprising, for Penguin, her mother, is one, and Woolly, Fathom's speckled merle son, is well on the way to becoming another.

Watch a dyed-in-the-wool *kannechor* at work and you will see a skill that puts all other canine skills to shame. Watch how, when he is with

77

you, walking around the farmyard of a hitherto friendly farmer, he ignores the poultry fluttering before him. No, ignores is not the right word. Watch how he deliberately goes out of his way not to notice those hens, turning his head lest he should see their inane, feathery hysteria. But beware this deceiver, this canine Judas Iscariot. Leave the poultry farm, walk away from its ricks and stock, but note how your dog shows a reluctance to come with you. Pretend not to notice the dog, take your eyes off its slinking, rolling gait. See how he inches back to the farmyard, see how exhilarated he becomes as he approaches his quarry, his belly nearly dragging in the grass, his legs bent like those of a cat ready to spring. Watch the almost ugly excitement that causes his body to quiver like a leaf in a spider's web, but, above all, watch the victim he has chosen, selected out of the flock of potential victims.

The chances are it will not be the hen feeding nearest to him, indistinguishable from the rest of the feeding poultry to your untrained eye. The chances are it will be a bird you have touched with your foot to move it out of your way, or a hen you have moved from its perch on a gate. Watch now, for this is the one he has singled out for his attentions as he slides towards it, more snake-like than dog-like, snatching up the bird with a single lunge, silencing its squawking by judicious pressure on its rib cage – pressure that is not enough to kill, but enough to drive all the air from its lungs so that its alarm cry dies in its throat. Then watch him high-tail it back for home, using every bush as cover, every wall, every shed, every obstacle to escape detection. The hen will still be alive when he drops it at your door, or worse still when the dog finds you in some lane, nuzzling your hand to make you take his treasure, making you

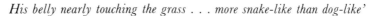

His belly nearly touching the grass . . . more snake-like than dog-like'

ashamed at your association with him, making you feel an unwilling Fagin to his enterprises.

How does one train a dog to become such an entrepreneur? How does one teach a dog to crawl twenty yards on its belly, freezing at every movement of its prey? Well, quite simply, these skills cannot be taught. Try to interfere with its *modus operandi*, amend its method of stealing, and the skill disappears or degenerates into something more sinister and decidedly ugly. Neither can you set out deliberately to breed a *kannechor*, for the skill, if skill it is, lies dormant in a strain, surfacing in the most unlikely of litters. Merle, for all his intelligence, for all his tractability, his willingness to please, was no *kannechor*, neither could he have been taught the skill, for Merle is an 'open' sort of dog, devoid of deceit. Fathom, a reluctant disciplinee, a difficult bitch to manage, a dog with a 'couldn't give a damn' attitude towards her owner, was a 'natural', a dyed-in-the-wool *kannechor*, as soon as this peculiar instinct slid like a summer butterfly out of the chrysalis of puppyhood and made ready to fly.

Fathom's thieving began insidiously, and perhaps, in a way, I must have thought her first attempts at robbery were funny. I live in an area famous for its wood pigeons and collared doves, birds that

Kannechor

multiply like rabbits and 'flock up' from the grit on the lane when a car approches them. At corn sowing, when barley or wheat is drilled, they are an unlovely aspect of the countryside, for flocks appear overnight and scratch up and wolf down the newly planted grain. Sadly, just as the corn attracts the pigeons, so do the pigeons attract the gunmen, and the fields behind my house become like scenes from a re-enactment of the battle of the Somme. Gunmen are particularly possessive by nature, and bitterly resent anyone encroaching on land they shoot. Indeed, in Lichfield, where I believe only recently has *droit de seigneur* been forgotten, trespass on a shoot attracts such a host of Panda cars that one would think they were raiding a 'Welcome Home Ronald Biggs' party. Such are the rigorously upheld rights of the shooting man, I suppose – a right that makes a pheasant more important than a person and the snatching up of a rabbit more worthy of police inquiry than a burglary. Well may our society favour the neutron bomb, a bomb that destroys a man's flesh and bones yet leaves his suit intact.

Well, with corn sowing finished, along came the usual gunmen, complete with camouflaged jackets and plastic effigies of wood pigeons to attract the careful woodies.

Normally, I don't exercise Fathom, though Merle is kept to a very strict routine, both with exercise and training. Fathom, however, is turned loose, and her sycophantic attentions on my neighbours usually result in her being crammed with all sorts of unsuitable food. If the food offerings do not materialize, however, dustbins will be emptied and their contents scattered like the workmanship of a dustman who has not received his Christmas tip. Normally, I do not allow her loose during the shooting, for in true Tom Lehrer style many of the shoot would not think twice about adding a lurcher to the game bag (twelve woodies, ten doves and a sort of 'brindled thing'), but after three days of non-stop gun-fire, I chanced it and turned her loose. She watched the ant-like figures at the sides of Taylor's field with interest, and then slunk off to Mrs Harrison's bin for any edible rubbish. But then, two or three times that day, she bumped the door with her head, and stood in the porch with a wood pigeon in her mouth. I dislike guns, I must admit, and the shoot are sufficiently aware of this antipathy to their sport as normally to keep away from my hovel. It was therefore all the more amazing when a short, stocky, middle-aged gunman, his face as red as a turkey cock, knocked at my door and began to yell abuse.

I stared back in astonishment, more fascinated by the vitriolic eloquence of the gunman than upset about any invasion of my privacy, but it was minutes before I could understand what he was

Fathom marking a rabbit-hole

saying. He gestured towards my porch, an unsightly affair, I admit, and pointed his gun ominously at my anorak lying on the floor of the porch and showing a few protruding feathers. Disdainfully he kicked my anorak aside – I've never been particularly clothes conscious anyway – to reveal a pile of very dead, lead-slain woodies, 'stolen', as my uninvited guest thundered, from his game bag. It was a delicate situation, my dislike of guns being known locally, but thank God, during a lull in the shouting Fathom appeared through a gap in the hedge opposite with yet another dove in her mouth. The gunman mumbled a few threats about prosecuted layabouts and dead lurchers, and his Rover roared off up the lane. I kept Fathom in next day, but the troubles had begun, for that evening she materialized in the porch with a partly cooked joint of beef – though how in hell she had obtained it is still open to speculation.

A week late, she bumped the door with her head and dropped a live rabbit in the porch. Nothing unusual about this. She often brought rabbits home. What *was* unusual was that it was a Dutch rabbit in prime condition, alive and with a show ring on its leg. At first I was not particularly upset about it as many rabbit owners turn loose their children's pets when the kids tire of them, as a glance at Barr Beacon by moonlight might indicate, but tales of vandals savagely tearing open heart-broken children's rabbit hutches slowly filtered back into the district, and once again I put Fathom under lock and key, at least until the heat was off.

Every person has something in his possession that he prizes above all other property, an object of his affection that excites the envy of others. In our district there lives a man called Richard Jacobbs. Yes, I'm right about the spelling – I've seen it often enough on his solicitor's letters. Richard's pride and joy is his poultry, a well-kept, pretty bunch of evil-looking Muscovy ducks, mallards, Pekin hens, but above all a team or two of tiny light Sussex bantams – neat white birds, whose necks are flecked with black hackles. They are attractive-looking poultry, though I'd not care to own any, mind you, and in the light of the rest of the story I think I should stress this point. Each day, when I walked three miles to catch a bus, I would pass Richard's garden and express my admiration for his poultry, and in time Richard and I developed a good relationship – that was, until Fathom came along.

Friday evenings are the time when most teachers, not totally cracked in the head, are glad that the next day is Saturday. My first tasks on arriving home are to put the kettle on, let Fathom loose for exercise and flop into a deep, school-free, exhausted sleep, a sleep free from disruptives, vandals and adolescent lunatics. That particular

Fathom on top form the day before the bantam incident

Friday was no exception. I let Merle and Fathom out and fell asleep. Two hours later, stiff and cold, I woke up and went out to feed the dogs. There was no sign of Fathom, and I went to bed uneasy about the prospect of her running loose all night, up to no good or dead in some field or other, the victim of the gunmen who infest our district now that Whittington has become a fashionable dormitory town for Birmingham.

Next morning saw no sign of her either, and I began to worry. I walked to the village that morning to fetch my pathetic supply of groceries. ('Do you live only on tea?' sneered the girl. 'You'll soon get to look like them apes.') At noon, I arrived back at the cottage to find Fathom lying on her belly in my porch, staring at my anorak, which lay, as usual, in the corner of the porch. From the folds of the anorak peeped the heads of three very frightened, very indignant light Sussex

Fathom marking one of Jacobbs' sitting bantam hens

bantams. Fathom continued to watch them intently, as a collie watches lambs, making a gentle warning *putt* at them as soon as they tried to leave the anorak. I suddenly realized how she must have spent the night, lying in the long grass ready and waiting for Jacobbs to let out his diminutive speckled birds, and then, as soon as Jacobbs had gone to his breakfast, snapping them up and heading for home. How she had kept them in the porch as she raced off for another baffled me, until I realized that, in a moderate wind, the door slammed as soon as it was touched.

I crated the poultry in an old Persil box and drove to Jacobbs's home in my dirty old van. I was desperately racking my mind for any alibi that would explain why I was in possession of his poultry, but none came, so I decided to tell him the truth. He was furious, of course, although his fury was tempered by amazement when he saw the birds unharmed, and he seemed almost regretful when he watched me thrash Fathom in the presence of his indignant little bantam trio. It's peculiar, but I believe she knew she'd done wrong. Like an alcoholic who is aware that a bottle will eventually kill, however, she just couldn't resist those tiny birds. Anyway, Jacobbs invited me into his cottage for tea, and a peculiar wine-like drink called metheglin, an infusion of herbs in a honey mead, and we talked of 'country matters', carefully avoiding the subject of bantams, lurchers and *kannechors*. I was slightly dazed with a burning sensation in my nostrils as I walked back to my van. Fathom was in the back, sulking at the one and only thrashing I had given her, for no other reason than to please Jacobbs, for I do not honestly believe violence does anything to help correct faults in dog or child. I drove off, my head still fuzzy with the one glass of that strange, antique liquor, but then my attention was attracted by a slight movement from beneath the passenger seat. Three feathered heads protruded: those of a cock and two hens.

I never let Fathom out again by herself. There was too much at stake, and I should be unhappy to be forced to disband my little canine menagerie. But now I must return the reader to the tale of Merle, who had by this time recovered from his injuries.

10 *Penguin*

It's funny, but I can't manage to remember the time when I didn't have Penguin. She seems always to have been with me, and nowadays, when lurchers are traded like Hudson Bay barter vouchers, that must be a novelty. She's a brindle bitch, a bit baggy in the belly now and grey muzzled like any fourteen-year-old bitch, but during her youth she was beautiful. From an ugly puppy, shapeless and a bit gauche, she changed overnight into a raging beauty. I suppose it's the same with most livestock. One day they're ugly-duckling caterpillars, the next they are beautiful swan imagos. Penguin was, in her heyday, with her superb nose, good catching ability and an aptitude to predict the ways of fur or feather, the nearest thing to a complete lurcher I've seen. All in all, it's a damned shame that such an animal has to grow old. She was famous in her youth as well, so

Penguin

famous, in fact, that one day I found two Irish tinkers in the run, looking at the dogs – uninvited, needless to add.

'Is der little bitch for sale, sir?' the younger one asked.

I groaned inwardly, knowing what would happen next, and a week later away went the caravans and following night away went Penguin. I wrote an article entitled 'The Least Efficient Public Service' about the efforts made by the police to retrieve my bitch, but decided against publication, partly because of the hassle it would cause and partly because Penguin turned up on my doorstep a week and a half later, footsore and starving but home never the less. I was glad to have her back, very glad, for at the time of the theft she was carrying the puppy I would later call Fathom, and to imagine Fathom having been born on some of those tinker sites would be unthinkable.

I had considered going rough with Penguin, going on the road in a real old gipsy vardo, for she could have easily poached enough to keep a man in meat if not in veg. Could! Well, once could have is the correct phrase, for she is long past catching hares and rabbits. But during her youth, when professional harassment in my job grew intense and I was deliberately phased out of the timetable in a move to make me desperately unhappy (a standard punishment for teachers who don't conform), I leaned heavily on Penguin, treating her as an insurance policy in case things went wrong, knowing I could live on the catches of this bitch if things went really sour in teaching.

As Penguin's speed faded, however, her ferocity grew, and she became quite a fearsome old tyrant, joining in every terrier battle in the run and behaving more like a terrier than a lurcher. And if she was no longer nippy enough to sort out rabbits and hares, she became a very devil on foxes. She met her first after Beltane had flushed it out of a copse, and though she coursed it, I felt she was not really trying as she would had a hare got up. Yet as she passed over it, it bowled and struck at her, putting in two deep fang cuts, in her face. It was an error, a ridiculous mistake, for had it not retaliated I think she would have allowed it to escape. As it was she came to life. She leaped back at the first encounter and then, screaming like a banshee, rushed in and seized the fox across the loins – not the best grip, as she was to discover, but twenty minutes after life had left its body she was still shaking that fox, lying down panting between sessions, blood running from the nips in her face as she renewed the struggle in paroxysms of rage. After that, she was wed to fox for life, and coursed them with great enthusiasm, never allowing them to make the first move.

She was a devil in the run, and most of the terriers avoided her as far as they could. Only Vampire dominated her or was allowed to eat a meat ration near her. The infant Merle was bowled flat by her once, and ever after gave her a clear berth. Furthermore, in spite of her age – and running dogs age rapidly after the age of seven – few dogs could better her in a skirmish. Still, she influenced Merle's development more than any dog I owned, partly because her remarkable nose triggered off his interest in hunting up rabbits – a craft of which I had eventually to break him – and partly because my owning her allowed Merle to see his first battle between fox and lurcher.

Winter had come with a vengeance, and against my better judgement I had mated Penguin to Terry Aherne's Rusty, allowing Mo, who was on his backside moneywise (no uncommon state for Mo or any of my friends), to rear and sell the puppies. She was, perhaps, two weeks pregnant, not pregnant enough to show, when I first took Merle out with her to go lamping across the neighbouring Dyatt estate. It was a good night for lamping: gusty, with the oak samplings nearly bending in the wind and rabbits a' plenty on the ground – squatters that even Penguin managed to take with geriatric lunges. But it was an evening completely free of foxes, right up until one o'clock, in fact.

At one o'clock we rounded a gateway that lead to the kale fields and flicked on the beam to a piece of land that could not have been more than twenty yards wide, a strip fenced in fine-gauge rabbit netting on one side and kale on the other. In the middle of the field, a pair of moon like eyes shone for just a second or so before the fox turned his head and became faintly visible in the beam. It was not a great period of time for a dog to make a decision, but it was enough for Penguin. I slipped her and she was on him in a trice, missing him with her first pass, bowling him once, but turning him off the kale and back towards the rabbit netting. She turned and ran him again, bowling him and overshooting, but was back on him again in a trice in earnest. He struck at her, but she feinted, avoided the bite and bowled him again. Then the battle against the rabbit wire started in deadly seriousness.

I slipped Merle, and like a rocket he hurtled towards the combatants. My heart skipped a beat at his enthusiasm. He bore down on the pair like the very devil, but just as he approached the struggling lurcher – shaking her fox, losing her grip and slipping in to get yet another hold – he stopped and began to view the spectacle, darting in yet seemingly fearing the outcome. Twice he came within a yard of the fight, and twice he retreated to a safe distance. At last I decided enough was enough, slipped in and finished the fight, killing the fox and putting Penguin on the slip. As soon as Penguin had been put up, Merle attacked the carcass of the fox like a fiend, shaking it by the

'The darkness was alive with huge luminous eyes . . .'

throat as a terrier shakes a rat. My disappointment at his not joining in the battle was somewhat eased by his enthusiasm for the worry, for quite a few dogs are undecided about what to do with their first fox carcass.

I returned home more exhilarated than depressed, and lay in front of the fire for the few remaining hours of the night. At school the next day I wrote up a cryptic note in my diary: 'He will I think make a *fairly good* fox killer for he has *some,* enthusiasm for the game'; but I was tempting providence. Next night, another moonless night, I walked the Dyatt estate at 1.35, rolling my car the last two hundred yards down the lane lest I disturbed the feeding foxes, confident that tonight I would see Merle commit mayhem on them and my van laden down with cadavers for the journey home.

It was a dreadful night, however, a night that caused bitter disappointment and a plummeting of spirits like I have rarely experienced. The darkness was alive with huge, luminous eyes, each one appearing as big as a saucepan lid in the lurid light of the beam, but most stayed out of reach, on the very limit of the beam, circling us, amazed and perhaps amused at the lunatic shining a light around the field. At 4.30 traffic began to build up on the road near the estate.

Foxless, I turned to walk back to the van, Penguin fractious and spiteful, with Merle chopping at him, front lips lifted every time the narrow path caused Merle to rub against her. He had always been afraid of her, always prepared, at feeding time, to relinquish his piece of meat if she so much as looked at him, and now I found him hanging back, reluctant to bring his head near to her jaws as we walked down the path to Dyatt's winter barley field.

I flicked the light once more. Two eyes lit up in the darkness, and before they could move I slipped Penguin. It was an easy slip, scarcely twenty-five yards of a slip on a dark night at a bewildered, dazzled fox, the sort of slip that would enable a fox terrier, let alone a lurcher, to catch a fox. Penguin made no mistake. She careered into it, bowling it, pinning it, shaking it. I then slipped an almost hysterically excited Merle, who was in the process of throwing cartwheels at the end of his slip. He took off like a bullet, but braked quickly as he came up to the battling pair and hung back, darting at the grapplers a full three feet outside the striking range of the fox. His cowardice was obvious, and I felt an icy block twist in my gut. For nearly two years I had lauded the intelligence of this dog and lived only to train him, only to watch him become an indifferent rabbiting dog, a ridiculously poor hare-coursing dog, and now to see him put on this display of crass cowardice. Penguin persisted with the battle, taking bite after bite after bite as she endeavoured to finish the fox, but Merle continued to dart in and out of the fray, terrified of venturing into the battle zone.

I think I felt an ugly anger as I slipped in and killed the fox, leashing up Penguin and throwing down the still twitching but very dead body of the fox. Merle attacked it with fury, biting and ragging it, lifting it clear of the ground and shaking it until he nearly shook himself off his feet. I can remember saying, 'It's great now it's dead, you cowardly sod. You weren't so keen while it was alive, were you?' I leashed him and headed for home to bathe Penguin's lacerations.

It would be nice to say that slowly but surely I coaxed Merle over this strange alien cowardice until he became a superb fox-catching lurcher. It would also be untrue. At that moment I came close to the stage I call 'Lurcher for sale ready for starting' or the less mercenary 'Free to a good home'. In short, I packed up training him, mentally wrote 'Quitter' against his name and vowed it would be the last time I would run him or take him out. I can remember locking his pen and hissing, 'You useless bastard,' as I flung in his portion of tripe feeling resentment that such a dog should eat up good, expensive food. My feelings towards him came as close to hatred as I could manage to feel about a dog, and at that moment I felt almost a sort of sympathy with

Lamping dog run off a slip

the man who beats a recalcitrant spaniel half to death, a spaniel on which he has lavished everything only to have it disgrace him at a shoot. Penguin was old, yet still game enough to tackle fox, and in her youth she had been a treasure at rabbiting and a very useful hare dog. Merle was seemingly good at nothing. He was not fast enough to take hares, not nimble enough to catch rabbits, not game enough to tackle a fox. He was a far cry from my complete lurcher, but close to becoming the most useless dog I've ever owned.

The First Fox

Life in my stretch of country is governed by the seasons – not by the artificial dimensions imposed by a calendar, but by climatic changes. Some years ago, when I used to walk each day from Lichfield, carrying a hundredweight sack for three long, weary miles, I looked forward to the appearance of the first leaves, the May leaves as they are called in this district, mute testimony to the fact that summer was coming. Likewise, the first leaf fall heralding winter caused dismay and depression, for like the grasshopper in the Aesop fable, winter always finds me unprepared, the leaking roof not fixed and the chimney still needing repointing.

The winter of 1980 saw another type of depression, however – a financial depression, an industrial decline that put one in every two lads out of work. School became more meaningless than ever, and even the kids who accept the potpourri of useless information served up under the guise of education began to see that, however well they understood David Copperfield or the social implications of building

One day they will finally swallow up my countryside under a concrete hell

the Coventry flyover, they would still leave school to join the dole queue. Useful boys, industrious lads who would make any firm glad to employ them, kicked their heels in Walsall, or at weekends walked the twelve m les to my cottage just for something to do. It was even worse for my black lads, my Sikhs and my Pakistanis, who were, in spite of TV documentaries to the contrary, well aware that there was no hope of them getting a job. As I stood up in class I felt ashamed of giving careers lessons when there were no jobs whatsoever for any of our boys. Each night I had to drive to the gates of the school and tell some of my godchildren, children of parents of all races who trusted me to look after their kids, that I could not find them work.

A monetary-oriented government is all very well, I suppose, and might be for the best. Unlike dad, I find politics little short of bewildering. Yet it was agony to see useful, bright lads of all creeds floundering in a slough of despond, facing a future of no hope. Secretly I began to envy Ephraim Pride and Alex Downton for whom no depression existed and for whom every day was like another. Each day I began to feel more ashamed of the worldly goods, pathetic worldly goods, I had amassed during my forty-three fruitless, rather meaningless years on this planet.

A spate of strange, outlandish crimes began to sweep the Midlands. A friend went down for not so neat a piece of deer poaching in Attingham. Local farms began to lose sheep to lurcher men from the near-by town. At shows, dogs capable of pulling down sheep were brazenly advertised. The police put the sheep thefts down to the poverty imposed by the depression, but boredom more than poverty was the cause of sheep and deer poaching. Crime rocketed and the lead ridge of my roof – I'd found the lead by digging in a rubbish dump, so perhaps there was some divine retribution in the theft – disappeared one night, sadly missed but undetected as usual. Hennessey, an aged Irish tinker – settled, but only in a sense, for few tinkers are ever really settled – upped and took to the road, ripping the copper boiler out of his council house and selling it as a sort of two-fingered gesture towards the council who had settled him. Civilized life had wrecked him, he said, broken his constitution. 'Wrecked his guts' was the expression he used, and that last winter on the road he died, aged eighty-eight, the last fluent-speaking adept of the Romany dialect known as *Bealagair na saer*, a form so complicated, so convoluted that it defeated John Sampson, the greatest modern linguistic expert in the language of the last totally free people.

The life Hennessey chose – curiously it transpired that, like a dying Viking, he wished to be floated out to sea at the end – had much to commend it. It was a life where material wealth meant very little and all that counted was the fact that life must be lived to the full, not harnessed to social conventions, not trammelled in the trappings of respectability. A Persian poet – I'm getting old, ten years ago I could have recalled his name – once wrote, 'Wealth is simply a glittering burden designed by Allah to break the back of the avaricious.' I know what he meant. Not all my friends have felt the same – though in the light of subsequent events perhaps I should take a long and critical look at the term 'friends'.

In the autumn, my 'friend' John Cope went on short time – two days a week to be exact. Every other day would find him waiting for me at my cottage as I drove up, engine clanging and soul groaning. His presence had begun to drive me nearly mad, and I grew frustrated at the loss of every evening spent in his company, a frustration that I experience when some fool who has read a book asks not to come hunting with me but simply to waste a day 'looking at my dogs'. Once one passes forty, not only does one seek to avoid mirrors, but each day grows more precious, each wasted moment more of a tragedy.

For conversation, John is a non-starter, and while I welcome interesting people to my house, people like John, people whose only comments are bored indictments of the way the world is misusing them, are deadly bores. I think he must once have done me a favour, though for the hell of me I can't remember it, but to clinch the relationship he asked me to be godfather to his daughter. As a rule I had seen him about once a year, which was as much as I could stomach, but after he went on short time and then, worse still, became redundant, he made my life a hell. Before he took up with me I was half-way to becoming a recluse. By the time he was finished, he had me yearning for my own exclusive company.

But still, he did contribute to the writing of this book, for without him I would never have ventured out on those hellish, freezing, sleet-drenched, frost-bitten nights, and without him Merle would probably still be a failure, sitting in No. 4 kennel, unentered, untried and probably unwanted, waiting for someone to offer 'a well-disciplined dog a good and permanent home'. It was an ill wind, I suppose, but I couldn't face another winter like that one. Come to think of it, neither could Merle, for Merle suffered most from John's interests. Now, when I look at the dog, his stitched-in tongue giving his face an odd, half-witted look, his absence of lips inviting comment on him as a rather ugly conversation piece, his ribs fractured and knotted to-gether until they resemble the feel of a Catholic rosary, I wonder whether he particularly thanks John for that awful winter.

I'd joked a great deal about the 'phloxes and those who swim in the

First snows and a hard punishing run

water' incident in the Chinese restaurant, the whole business being made even more hilarious by the TV showing of *The Water Margin*, a Japanese-made Chinese soap opera with English dubbing that came out with such wonderfully cryptic if totally baffling little aphorisms as, 'Do not pity the ant because it is smaller than the sperm whale, he is also smaller than the peony' – comments that sounded good at the time but left one baffled half an hour later. I'd never really considered selling foxes however – fresh caught and oven read, so to speak – until John came up one Friday with his brilliant idea. Well, it was brilliant for him, since he didn't have to do the work or take any more than a casual interest in the business.

'Cobbledicks,' he said, referring to a concern that bought skins and animal bric-à-brac, were offering twenty quid a skin for foxes – 'Twenty quid!' he repeated, as if astounded at the stupidity of any firm prepared to throw away good money on the hides of foxes. 'Jesus,' he added, 'I've just looked in your ferret pen. You've got three in there with skins. Sixty bloody quids' worth. Sixty quid!' he repeated, staggered at the standard of cuisine I was prepared to feed my ferrets. 'It bloody nigh broke my heart.' And he then proceeded to explain how tough life was on the dole and how my goddaughter needed new shoes, sounding a bit like a Damon Runyon craps player ('Baby needs a pair of shoes').

I explained to him how hard hunting foxes would be, how icy the nights could be, how soul-destroying the failures, how dangerous an occupation is poaching foxes, but he has always regarded me as an effete schoolteacher (''S not a man's job really, is it?'), incapable of toil and exaggerating the hardship of a night's hunting. ('Christ, Bri, you wouldn't know what a day's work is like.') Inexorably I felt myself sliding into a partnership with him: me catching, me skinning; him selling, him keeping. Yet hard as I tried to stop the ill-fated alliance, by the end of the evening I found myself agreeing to let him hunt with me and keep the pelts. After all, I had at the most two weeks' work left in Penguin before she whelped her litter of pups to Grip, and since Merle was useless I had little to lose. Two weeks of leisure time at the most, I estimated.

Subsequently, Sunday night ('Ner, Bri, not Saturday. Saturdays is beer night, and I'm not missing the only bit of pleasure I get') found me, lamp in hand and feet on someone else's land, after foxes with Penguin and, as an after-thought, Merle, brought along as a rather useless ornament to watch the sport. Fox pelts were priced highly at that time, and fox pelts only command a good price during freezing weather when the fur is thickest and moult halted. The night was the most typical of the season: a light snow and a biting wind, the sort of

First fox

wind that cuts one to the marrow and drives all good hard-drinking men home to their beds. Or so I hoped, for I was already weary of John's company, his infernal bleating about how the world was treating him, his references concerning his macho, womanizing image and his ability to consume an enormous quantity of Ansell's beer, slurping it down like a pig.

As I looked at him, as I flicked on the beam, illuminating his shivering, complaining face, I suddenly felt determined he would be tested to the full that night, exhausted to the point where he was too tired to boast about how he had nearly had a trial for 5th team Warley Rugby Club and out of breath and too frozen to sing a pointless ditty about an unfortunate girl called Mollie who did amazing things to all the Llanelli rugby team, reserves as well (you must know the song, Bri, you're Welsh'). I hate this sort of person who thinks that my reluctance to frolic naked in the showers with numerous overweight, glutinous rugby-playing cherubs brands me as peculiar. He was no countryman, no person to fit in with my way of life, merely a man out to make a not so fast buck, out to exploit my land, my dogs, my toil, and, what was worse, to waste my leisure. From time to time the silence was broken by hissing whispers of, 'Christ, it's cold,' and I felt a warm glow of satisfaction bathe me, making me forget the hardship of the night.

It was pitch-black when we reached Thorpe's place, a small wood that bordered on to a midden pile littered with chicken cadavers, and we crouched waiting for the land to settle and the breath coming from Cope's lungs like a steam engine to quieten.

'Hell, I didn't think it would be like this,' he moaned.

'It isn't. Sometimes it gets quite bad,' I said quietly. 'It also gets boring,' I added as a discouraging afterthought.

At 1.30 I felt my legs becoming uncomfortably numb and glanced at my watch. I flicked the lamp around the pile and picked up five sets of eyes gazing back at me: a vixen and four cubs, perhaps, or simply foxes forced into this area by inclement weather, bad hunting or persecution from the two neighbouring hunts, which hunt right up to the borders of this poultry farm.

An easy slip, a certain catch, and I hissed, 'Let her go,' to John. 'Now!' I added, for his tardiness in slipping was obvious.

The dog raced along the beam and struck at the nearest fox, pulling it over, throwing it, trying to pin it, throwing it again and finally losing it as it slipped over the top of the midden pile into darkness and safety. So fascinated was I with the lightning run-up, the catch, the throws and even the fox's dextrous use of the dark side of the mound, that it was a full minute before I realized that there, raring to go, still

Fox no. 66

on the slip and doing cartwheels in excitement was Penguin. John had by the merest chance, the most odd of mistakes, slipped Merle, my failure, the dog that I'd only taken along for the ride.

I sat down on my haunches in amazement while Merle trotted back, shaking his head to ease a stinging bite on his muzzle. He sat quietly behind us, allowed John to replace the slip and me to check the bite – a tiny but deep puncture – without a murmur. Suddenly my foolish, gauche, cowardly dog had awakened and come to life. True, he had missed his first fox, but I've run twenty foxes in an evening without catching one, so I wasn't disappointed. He'd made a try, shown he was no quitter, justified his keep, but on the next slip, when I sent Penguin to get another feeding yearling, he once again darted around the periphery of the battle, snapping but refusing to go in to help the old bitch.

It took me three hours to understand what was wrong. Merle was not afraid of foxes. Far from it. Merle was afraid of Penguin!

12 *It's a Have and Have-Not World, I'm Afraid*

Merle never looked back, as the saying goes, and we began to take foxes fairly regularly with him. He suffered badly at first. In fact, during his first real catch, a catch he held in spite of a heated battle, he took a severe pasting. We were hunting the land 'twixt Whittington and Lichfield – an area now 'properly hunted', so some members of the British Field Sports Society tell me, so we are no longer invited there to lamp the foxes – and he ran down the beam, grabbing the fleeing fox as it moved out of the corridor of light. He 'muffed' his catch bowling it, and then, rather than let it escape, snatched and caught it across the loins. The result was predictable. It turned, spitting like a cat, and retaliated by puncturing him badly, causing a low whimper to escape from Merle's mouth, a whimper discernible nearly thirty yards away. He released the fox, shaking his head as he did so, but straight away made after it again, bowling it as it made for the hedge near the big brook.

When I came on him, he was holding the fox in a throat hold, a hold that made its furious struggling and spitting impotent. It was a hold that he learned to perfect, a hold that seemed as scientifically planned, perhaps, as a lock by Hackenschmidt. After that, throughout that long and freezing winter, he was rarely badly torn during the hunt. His technique was simple but efficient. His collie dam gave him brain enough to learn this strategy, and from his greyhound sire came lightning-quick reflexes, the ability to feint at a foe, avoid the counter-stroke and then topple the victim. He would run up the beam of light, sometimes taking an aeon of time to choose the correct moment to make his bid, often driving me to a frenzy with his tardiness in coming to grips with the quarry – the tardiness I first equated with cowardice. Yet when he deemed the moment was right, and only then, he would shoulder charge, bowl his fox and pin it with that inexorable throat hold, bowling it, turning it over a dozen times, flinging it, but pinning it with a hold that prevented retaliation. Oh, he missed foxes, it is true, but what dog, running down a searchlight beam over rough country, through bracken, against hedges, through brooks and through slurry, over midden piles, through unspeakable filth can have a hundred-per-cent record? Only an idiot would boast such results, and only an idiot would believe such tales.

He learned lamping so quickly that it was incredible, but then all first-cross collie greyhounds seem to take instantly to the sport, although, as I've mentioned, the tremendous noses of first crosses can be a problem for the lamper. After his first lamping session, however, Merle became aware that he must watch the beam of light. He instantly seemed to know that when we were out after fox he must not try for rabbits. It would be poetic to say that slowly but surely he overcame his need to sniff out quarry, but it was not so. He learned to ride with my peculiarities and I learned to tolerate his idiosyncrasies. It was a matter of a night or so before he became completely uninterested in the scent beneath his feet as soon as the beam flashed on, but on exercise days, days when, owing to my own idle nature, I would turn him loose in the field behind my cottage, he would run nose down on a hare scent or run rabbits up and down the hedgerow like a pocket beagle. As soon as night fell and the artificial light began to play around the field, however, the land might just as well have been devoid of scent so far as he was concerned. In short we became, as they say in the very best women's magazines, *sympatico*.

In the early mornings, when I returned from those exhausting hunts, I knew that, tired as I was, he must be more so, for an ordinary dog during a casual exercise period is supposed to travel three times as far as a man. Who can calculate the distance a lurcher runs during a hard night's lamping, however, particularly when the run terminates in a head-on tackle, a skirmish that can continue for up to a minute, a minute that must seem like a lifetime of exhausting battle to the antagonists. True, I never allowed him to kill his fox, not for any humane reasons, though a to-the-death struggle 'twixt a lurcher and a fox is a fairly nasty and bloody business, but simply because a fox so killed, a fox that has died by a strangling hold or simply a series of savage bites and shakings, usually has an unsaleable skin, a hide that resembles a chapel lady's moth-eaten tippet. Furthermore, he needed all the help he could get, for we were hunting for gain, not to see a *Quo Vadis?* sort of struggle, a macabre spectacle like something from Fitzbarnard's curious book *Fighting Sports*. After a run and a catch, he would flop down exhausted, but within minutes would be ready and more than willing to try again. But it was a grindingly hard soul-destroying winter for both of us.

Meanwhile, pelt hunters came under fire in the sporting press. Letters were written to the editors by blimp-like cartoon figures who give substance to my communist father's theory that Britain's

I had to carry Merle home after this one

military greatness was due to the expendability of the 'thin red line' rather than intelligent leadership. We, the pelt hunters, were accused of spoiling sport, allowing our kills to be skinned and the hide sold rather than letting hounds tear the carcass to pieces as all good sportsmen should! We were called unsporting by those who considered that only those who rode to hounds hunted, the rest of us just playing around like Bengali peasants, being allowed to snatch up a few sporting crumbs from the tables of the hunting artistocracy. I read the letters in wonder, amazed at the lack of perspicacity in an editor of a sporting periodical who allowed the field-sport fraternity to be divided into the haves and the have-nots at a time when all hunting is under fire and no chink in the armour should be left for public opinion to stamp out man's hunting imperative. At shows I met several of these blimps and breathed a sigh of relief, for they were a dispirited, bored and boring sect who, should they be used as an advertisement for Yeastvite, would ensure the firm went bankrupt. I read the letters, laughed a little at the writers' ponderous attempts at lucidity and ignored them. Each dead moon continued to find me abroad after foxes.

Our number of catches rose and the hides drying on Cope's shed grew rapidly in number. After forty skins were dried, he sold them and kept the money for himself not even paying my vet's bills, bills which I paid out of the 'phlox' money from Chinese restaurant owners who paid such a hell of a price that they must have eaten the foxes themselves rather than serve them up as Fox Foo Yung or sweet and sour fox. As winter progressed, accounts of prosecutions for poaching began to appear more regularly in the local and national papers. The *Shooting Times* published an article about a pair of men caught with a rabbit and fined £240, because not only were they caught in possession of a 'stolen' coney, but one of the men had been armed with a sheath knife. 'In possession of an offensive weapon,' the charge probably read. It looked a stinging fine for what I considered a bit of a trumped-up charge.

Poaching is theft, I suppose, but there are far worse crimes that are treated as jokes in magistrates' courts. My resentment at the in-equality of the law, of social codes that found quaint 'poaching' verses by Patrick Chalmers acceptable or at tweedy ladies who quoted, between giggles and appreciative laughter, Richard Monkton, 1st Lord Houghton:

> On the first of September one Sunday morn
> I shot a hen pheasant in standing corn,
> Without a licence!—contrive who can
> Such a cluster of crimes against God and man!

and then considered a £240 fine for a coney to be a fair and just sentence. I seethed with bitterness, a bitterness made worse by an article which appeared the same day, an account of a skinhead hell bent for trouble who beat up an elderly man and received probation for his crimes. Probation! It is regarded as a joke by the lads in the district where I teach, thought of as the equivalent of having a case dismissed, for even appearance at the probation office is considered to be 'optional' by many thugs.

I can remember becoming incensed with fury at the division of property and privilege in our country, and of the feudalistic laws that allowed such incredible travesties of justice. In my youth our house must, at various times, have held just about every communist and anarchist in Europe, guests of my incredible Marxist father, besotted

Three 'phloxes' for the Chinese restaurant

with politics, who was not quite energetic enough to go out and make a better world. As I grew up, like St Paul I put away childish things and rejected his teachings as unrealistic. Now, with my forty-second birthday rapidly looming on the calendar, I began to consider that dad could have been correct and that our green and pleasant land was truly in the hands of mindless plum-in-the-mouth rulers, all frantic to deal out fire, death and destruction for any of the *hoi polloi* like me who dared to violate their rigid class structure by hunting.

As my feeling of resentment grew, I no longer continued to hunt land on which I had permission but ventured further afield, trespassing not only on land where not only I had no permission, but venturing on to farms where the owners were positively hostile to me and would certainly not only prosecute but whose relatives and aquaintances sat on the bench and would deal out my punishment if I became careless and got caught. I was hunting foxes for skins in country hunted by fox-hound packs whose task is supposedly to keep down foxes on the land they hunt. Yet, should I assist them in their task and take a fox or two to sell its skin or carcass and be careless enough to get caught, I would almost certainly be charged with being in possession of rabbits and not foxes, for the taking of rabbits carries a stiffer fine. Should I be foolish enough to carry a penknife to skin my foxes, or a club to kill them, then I would certainly be charged with being in possession of an offensive weapon. Poachers with sense in fact shed any knives, clubs, belts and so forth as soon as they realize their collars are being felt.

I began to have sympathy with the old poacher of Lilias Rider Haggard's *I Walked By Night*, or the oddly politically orientated anti-hero of Hawker's *Victorian Poacher*, and while my education, my professional training, taught me that what I was doing was criminal, I felt that my forays on to the forbidden land of hostile people were blows for freedom. 'You are now taking the first steps to becoming middle class by becoming a teacher,' said a quaint old headmaster for whom I once worked, but his middle class was staid, well behaved and orthodox, and perhaps devoid of any feeling or rebellion against the status quo. My own middle class, the middle class of Orwell, was turbulent, indignant at injustice and ultimately revolutionary, but my bitterness against the way the landed gentry treated my kind and my attempts to strike a blow for my class brought me to grief. Cue for the story of 'The Boar at Hagger's Wood' − now read on. There's no politics in the rest of the book. That's a promise.

13 *The Boar at Hagger's Wood*

Hagger's wood is eight miles from my cottage, and I should not have been there. Furthermore, I'd been warned off in no uncertain manner about even going near the place. I suppose I was tempting fate, but it would have been a very unadventurous sort of chap that could resist the challenge.

I don't particularly like Hagger and he hates me. He regards me as a poaching, dishonest lout and I look on him as a fat, obnoxious little blimp, a blimp that I find it impossible not to torment until he goes into paroxysms of rage, screaming and threatening death. He belongs in a bygone age, an age that regarded it as a privilege for a hunt to cross his lands, a pleasure to see his crops squashed flat by hounds and bowler-hatted hunters. Long after fox hunting has been abolished, I am sure I will still find this tubby little red-faced man touching his cap to anyone dressed in an expensive hacking jacket.

Hagger is not a happy man. He has few friends and tragedy seems to have pursued him through his life. Fourteen years ago, when I first came to live in the area, I heard a hideous tale of a mishap at Hagger's place. Hagger breeds Jersey cattle and a Jersey bull is a good enough reason for chickening out of poaching certain fields. The heifers look like Walt Disney cattle: doe-eyed, black-muzzled and cute. But the bulls are as vicious as hell, and next to a Spanish fighting bull must be up among the world's most savage cattle. Hagger had such a bull, a mean furious beast, half the weight of a Hereford but spiteful and unpredictable. Three weeks before it had pulverized a Mini that a terrified courting couple had driven into the field one night, so Hagger should have been ready for trouble. He wasn't, however, and sent his seventeen-year-old son down to take out an in-season heifer from the bull. An hour later, so the tale goes, the bull appeared at Hagger's farm with Hagger's son's sports jacket sleeve and an arm still in the sleeve. That's the tale, true or not, and it would be a ghoulish sort of person who would ask Hagger whether the story was fact or fiction. A week after the tragedy, his twelve-year-old daughter's pony shied and dragged the unhorsed girl three miles along grit-surfaced roads back to the farm. Hagger simply went around the bend, and who could blame him, so it must appear a shame to torment the poor chap the way we did. But to tell the truth, I just can't resist tormenting Hagger.

Hagger is absolutely convinced that I take pheasants off his farm, and to put the matter straight, I'd better say that I've never touched his damned pheasants. He is also adamant that I have run and killed foxes on his farm, a subject about which I shan't comment, and he never misses an opportunity to come over to me and rant and rave about what he intends to do to me if he catches me on his farm. If he is serious, and I have a horrid suspicion he is, men will talk about the manner of my death for a thousand years. He is also convinced I am an arsonist, a murderer and probably a sheep worrier, and my friends normally play up to his little tantrums and goad him on to attack me. (I can do without such friends.)

The night in question, John Cope and I called in at Hagger's local to buy a bread roll before lamping some land near Hagger's wood. We sat at the corner table and watched the drinkers, listening to their tales of ferrets, game cocks and poaching, all very exaggerated perhaps, but very entertaining. Then, into the bar rolled Hagger, red-faced, tiny, overweight and noisy – an advertisement for an incipient coronary, I've always thought. He settled among his cronies and began to talk loudly. John edged to the bar and ordered a drink.

'Any foxes on your farm, Mr Hagger?' he asked innocently.

Hagger went puce, but ignored John and strode over to me.

'You bastard!' he yelled. 'You bastard, leave them foxes alone. The foxes is the 'unts, that's what the 'unts are for, you, you bastard. I've seen you and that speckly' – it took me a minute to realize he meant Merle – 'on my land after foxes. I saw that speckly in your car, you boogar, I know what yer after. It's them pheasants, innit, you bastard? I'll bleeding kill yer if yer on my land. I'll shoot you and that speckly, shoot yer both bloody dead, I will, you and your speckly, you bastard,' he screamed.

'Well, it's very nice of you to give me permission to hunt your land, Mr Hagger. You want me to get rid of your foxes, you say?' I said loudly.

He gripped the table for support. 'I'll bleedin' kill you, I will, you boogar, you bloody boogar, yer bastard,' he screamed.

The landlord edged towards us. 'I think you two should leave while you still can,' he hissed. 'Things will get a bit rough if you don't.'

'Thanks for the permission, Mr Hagger,' I yelled as we went through the doorway. 'We'll get rid of all the foxes for you.'

'They're the 'unts, you boogar, let them alone,' he screamed.

But that night, out of pure devilry I decided to return to Hagger's wood, taking with me the lurcher known unaffectionately to Hagger as 'the speckly'. It was to be an interesting night, and that is an understatement.

I dropped John at home and parked my car in his gateway, walking the two miles back to Hagger's wood, lamp on back and 'speckly' on slip. Now, lamping is not a particularly dangerous activity, for a seasoned lamper only gets caught if he is careless or, worse still, gets lazy. Few police are gong to go out of their way to investigate a light shone around a field, unless the policeman owns a slice of the shooting rights and then, as like as not, he will spend quite a lot of time patrolling the area. If a police officer goes into the field to investigate, then all the lamper has to do is shut off the beam, whistle or click in his lurcher and, since most lamping is done on dark, gusty moonless nights, disappear without trace into the darkness. However, a car or even worse a van parked in the gateway is a death trap, especially an empty van, for all your bobby (or worse still your gamekeeper, for gamekeepers are extremely predatory fellows, as eager for blood as a young stoat) has to do then is wait by the car. Sooner or later, the mountain comes to Mahomet and gets caught.

It began to drizzle a fine spider's-web sort of rain that dampened rather than soaked as I reached Hagger's wood. Frankly, in spite of the jokes, Hagger's place wasn't a good hunting pitch for foxes, and I never knew a day when the hounds 'found' on his land. Even so, the old chap guarded his place for the hunt and guarded it zealously.

At Hagger's wood I slipped through the barbed wire, its tines twanging on my donkey jacket, and strode into the thicket, Merle as close to heel as a Barbara Woodhouse dog. Icy trickles of water dripped from the trees and ran down my neck, and being a bit of a fine-weather hunter, I considered heading for home after all. However, I shook off both the rain and the depression and climbed the fence into the field that led to Hagger's house. It was an act of brazen defiance to lamp those fields in front of Hagger's farmhouse, but even should hell have me, I had to do it. Yet on reflection, it wasn't particularly dangerous. In the event of a light coming on in the house, I could flick off the beam, disappear in the woods and high tail it for home. Furthermore, Merle is superbly disciplined and comes in on a click, so escape would be a damned sight easier than for someone who owned a recalcitrant sort of dog. Even so, I glowed with defiance at my courage in shining my beam over his fields.

I flicked on the lamp and flashed the beam around, hoping for a momentary glimpse of soup-plate eyes. As I suspected, there was nothing. I was about to give the field a lap of honour to annoy the old devil when a small bright eye flickered red in the thin beam of light. I moved the beam slightly, flickering it from side to side, to discern the shape and identity of the eye's owner. For a second I thought of roebuck – how stupid it must seem now – and during that second I slipped Merle. He ran down the outside of the corridor of light, came in from the side and struck at the eye. It moved slowly and cumbersomely, and Merle's second strike lifted the owner into the air, flinging it a few inches off the ground. A bag-like shape appeared in the beam, a shape at which Merle lunged again. I saw his head go in for the strike, and suddenly he shot backwards as though struck in the face by a hammer. Merle seemed to reel for a second and then ran in on the foe. Again he flung it and again he reeled from some counter-punch that all but threw him off balance.

The eye began to move then, and the beam picked up the ponderous ursine shape of the biggest badger I have ever seen. It was madness, stupid pointless madness, but for the life of me I could not switch off that beam and stop the battle. Merle ran in once more on the boar, now racing like a clockwork tortoise away from the wood towards the road, but this time he avoided the strike of the badger and simply slipped under the blow, lifting the badger and throwing it a few inches, rolling it off balance, slowing it up a little but not pinning it. Again he ran in, again he struck, but missed his hold and tottered back like a poled ox. Then, sin of sins, he began to bark at the fleeing shape.

I had never heard Merle even yap before then, and come to think of it, he never committed the cardinal sin again, but that night, running a boar badger across the most hostile territory (hostile to me and the 'speckly'), he bayed like thunder, barking fit to wake the dead, or if not the dead, at least to wake Hagger.

'You bloody fool, Merle,' I hissed, but it wasn't Merle who was the fool, but the man holding the lamp. At any time during the brawl I could have stopped the battle simply by calling in the dog, switching off the beam and leaving the field. Yet I allowed the pointless mauling to go on, and even endeavoured to turn the juggernaut back into the field as I would a hare, by rocking the lamp and flicking it off and on in an effort to slow up the boar's rolling, ponderous flight. It was a ridiculous display of stupidity, a man of close on forty-two years old trying to get a dog to catch a useless boar badger, a beast I would have released even if I had caught it, a beast whose skin I couldn't sell even as a curio. Furthermore, I am no newcomer to the world of badgers. I've kept terriers, had them mauled and killed by badgers, so I know exactly what the business end of the devil was doing to my lurcher and winced every time I saw that small piggy head dart out and connect with Merle. Worst of all, I allowed the battle to blot out

'. . . the ponderous ursine shape of the biggest badger I have ever seen . . .'

any sense of danger that I should have felt at lamping the ground of an enemy, for lamping a testing quarry, be it hare or badger, tends to mesmerize the hunter, making him totally involved in the course, allowing him to feel as though he is actually running alongside the dog, his heart and muscles often in unison with the aching parts of the lurcher. When lamping, the dedicated lamper is fooled into believing he is the only person left in the world and that the night belongs only to him – and brother, oh brother, that is a monumentally dangerous delusion.

I was snapped out of my reverie by the sound of a car, ignition turned off, quietly rolling down the hill. The human mind seems to function at two levels. Plane one is the obvious day-to-day function; the other is at a subconscious state, but keyed in enough to detect any threat of danger. There could be no other reason to explain how, in spite of the noise of Merle's barking, the badger snuffling and me running across ploughed land, I could have detected the faint sound. Perhaps herd beasts, beasts that are prey to predators, have this instinct to a far greater extent. Psychology and speculation aside, however, I flicked off the beam, clicked my fingers. Instantly the battle finished and Merle was by my side.

The rolling car came to an almost silent halt and I heard the faint click of a door opening and large but quiet feet coming up to the roadside gate. I froze and touched Merle to 'lie'. Quite suddenly, a weak rather pathetic beam began to play around the field, barely illuminating ten yards of land. Into the field two or three people (it was difficult to tell number) stepped as I remained stuck still, barely breathing, only fifteen feet away. I pressed hard into the hedge of thorn, ridiculously trying to blend with the landscape.

'He's here, occiffer, that bloody schoolly and his speckly, I know it. I seen his light. Him and his bloody speckly, he's here 'an had time to run, he's here. Catched him now,' he spoke almost triumphantly as if he actually knew I was hiding in the leeward side of his hedge. 'Got the boogar now, the bastard.'

'Doesn't seem to be anyone here now, Mr Hagger,' said a quiet voice, a voice that, as Moses says, shouts out loud 'Old Bill'. The 'occiffer' shone the lamp around the field once more, just for good measure, and then, with the note of resignation of a man torn from his sandwiches and flask of tea, he added, 'If you hear anything else, Mr Hagger, I'll be straight over. Just give us a ring.'

'The boogar, the boogar,' Hagger was chanting as they started up the engine and the car drove off towards Hagger's house on the hill.

I sat there petrified, my every fibre weak with fear, my legs shaky as jelly and my stomach fluids swishing around like a British Railway tea urn. I felt mildly sick and rather stupid, for I had risked prosecution at the hands of Hagger (and there was no chance of him not preferring charges, the boogar), just for a run at a badger – a badger I did not take. It was to be two hours before I could summon life back into my legs and will them to move. I lay in that hedge a good three hours before dawn began to break and I deemed it safe to go home. With care and stealth I crossed the main road a hundred yards from my hiding place to vanish into the woods opposite.

In the middle of the road lay a sack of sorts. I could scarcely discern its nature and contents in the dawn light, and against my better judgement walked towards it. The mound was no sack, however, but my badger, a huge boar, forty-nine pounds in weight, the biggest I've ever seen, and a victim of a car accident. I was baffled. I'd poached all the land for miles and there was no set large enough or worked enough to hold a badger for three miles in any direction. What

The boar at Hagger's End

curious event, what disturbance, had driven this ancient giant from his lair to stray across Hagger's land and finish his life in Hob Lane under a car? I dragged the colossus aside and hid him under the hedge, picking him up later during the daylight on my way to work.

Marilyn was an unwilling model for the photograph, and needed much persuasion to pose with the cadaver of a badger, believe me, but the beast was the biggest I'd ever seen. I had to photograph it to prove that such a beast could actually exist and that I did actually run it with Merle.

Merle himself was in no doubt that he had tangled with the veteran. Those broken brown teeth, those huge digging claws had played havoc. Merle's throat and jaws were badly bitten, and he carried his front leg for days before I realized his shoulder had been massively bruised. I felt rather ridiculous about the whole business and was irritated by John's comment, 'How much can you get for a badger skin? Do you think it's worth while hunting them full time?' I was even more angered by his exasperation when I told him Merle would be out of action for a week or more. All in all, it was a rather pointless night's hunting.

I was still thinking about the events at eleven o'clock next day during a cover lesson – when one of the more orthodox staff is away we eccentrics have to cover for them – but was snapped out of my reverie by Susan Clark, runny nosed and slightly violent, who pushed a piece of paper in front of me and said, 'Your dog, sir. Good, innit.'

The drawing, amateurish even for an eleven-year-old (Sue is sixteen), showed a curious-looking dalmatian-type animal with the bat ears of a Cape hunting dog.

'Write Speckly under it, Sue,' I said. 'It's lovely.'

I posted the drawing to Hagger. No signature, of course. I'm not that brave. But I'm sure he knew who had sent it – the boogar.

14 'No, Send the Little Fat One, I Want It Done Properly'

I have favourite people in my life, people who do not annoy me even when they arrive half-way through me writing a book, people who are a far cry from the 'Just called to see you, Bri' people who arrive on Sundays or, strangely, during my very infrequent baths. Dennis Abbott, breeder of fighting cocks, teller supreme of weird and earthy Black Country stories, is one of those favourites. He can arrive when I am half-way through writing the most critical chapter of a book without having me bang my head on the table in despair at the intrusion. Dr John Harpur is another, an expert with a blow gun, a length of highly polished copper piping that can project a dart made out of a cotton-wool pad warheaded with a sharp heavy darning needle deep into an oak door with a quick goldfish-like gulp of his mouth. Highly entertaining, but hell on stately oak doors. The person of whom I speak now, however, is Mr Stone, another favourite person in spite of the fact that he is affectionately known to our group as The Death Angel, a nickname I had best explain, and explain quickly.

Stone is a smallholder, one of those 'tiny' farmers who eke out a somewhat precarious living from a piece of land that wouldn't produce enough money to keep a major landowner in bootlaces. Stone's place is immaculate, a series of well-kept battery houses and free-range arks of neat, newly cleaned pigsties and well-kept calves fattening in a field surround by a walled garden. So how come the nickname? Stone brought a bitch to be mated to Vampire some two years ago, and sensing a fellow down-on-his-luck type of person, as broke as I was or am, I waived the fee.

'If you have something that dies, drop it in for the dogs,' I shouted as he drove away – a comment inviting disaster, or 'wishing it', as Moses calls it. For the next two weeks, disaster after disaster struck at the poor devil's livestock and bags of hen cadavers were regularly dropped at my door by a doleful-faced Mr Stone. Scarcely a day went by without some 'unfortunate' being fed to my dogs. One day I invited him in for tea.

'I've got me son in the back of the van,' Stone apologized so as not to accept my offer.

'My God,' uttered Roger. 'Not him dead as well.'

'Death Angel' nickname explained. As I've said, Mr Stone is one of my favourite people, and next I think I'd better explain what is meant by the term a walled garden.

The reign of George III wasn't a particularly pleasant time in which to live if one was poor, but for those with money it was just dandy. Fairytale castles called follies sprouted like mushrooms all over the country, simply as an expression of someone who wished to show the world he had money to burn. Walled gardens, expensive four-acre and five-acre enclosures, were built to house vegetable plots. They were not particularly effective methods of keeping out pests as the eccentric rich frequently allowed half-tame hares to rampage in their enclosures, which inspired poets, perhaps, but couldn't have helped the cabbages all that much. The walls were elaborate affairs, cunningly constructed with fireplaces built into them every few dozen yards and an elaborate system of flues connecting the fireplaces. Thus fires could be lit, the walls warmed and peaches and nectarines grown against the wall and ripened even when there were late frosts. Money isn't everything, but what it isn't it can buy, as the saying goes.

Stone's wall

Mr Stone has no such delusions of grandeur, however, and cattle and pigs now feed where hares once lived out their incarceration, for Stone rented the holding long after the estate had been divided up and the deaths of its peach-obsessed inhabitants. Still, it is a fascinating relic of a bygone age, much appreciated by admirers of the Croesus-like wealth of the eighteenth-century aristocrats. I am, however, not an antiquarian, in spite of my curiously crumpled looks. My interest in the wall is in the fact that it houses a host of animals ranging from rabbits with a finely developed sense of the precarious to badgers.

Foxes also hole up in the walls, particularly in bad winters, entering and leaving via the fireplaces like vulpine Santa Clauses. Indeed, six years ago, several litters of cubs were reared in the place, but since then badgers have taken over and no vixen has littered there, for badgers are highly omnivorous and find newly born fox cubs better as food than as fellow tenants. Yet the area is thick with foxes, and cubs bred in the sanctuary of Broughs Earths invariably hole up at some time in their lives in the walls surrounding Stone's enclosed garden. Now foxes at the bottom of the garden are great if one is an urban dweller who delights in seeing out-of-place mammals near his home, but if one is a poultry farmer, they are certainly not that much fun. Mr Stone had taken some fairly hefty 'stick' from the foxes that lived in the flues that honeycombed his wall, and this, after a very long, circuitous route, brings us to the point of my story.

Mr Stone is a reasonable sort of chap and Mick and Roger enjoyed quite a bit of sport messing around Mr Stone's holding, chasing the odd rat or even an occasional rabbit with their terrier and Bedlington whippet lurcher. Very soon, however, Mr Stone began to lose hens to the foxes, one or two hens at first, but quite a few as the months went by and the foxes got the hang of his place. Not unnaturally, he was not exactly pleased. So he asked the lads to stop the depredations. Easier said than done.

First, Toby, Mick's terrier puppy, was only seven months old, Roger's lurcher was only a shade older. Next, the nature of the wall was a very real problem. Stone had had his own terrier jammed in the wall only the year before, and it had certainly caused some trouble. It is damned nigh impossible to dig out a trapped terrier from such a place, even with the inevitable Fell and Moorland club rescue team. So it was that Mick and Roger put snares down in every conceivable (and to tell the truth every inconceivable) place. The results were somewhat less than satisfactory, which must rank as one of the understatements of the century.

Next morning, we checked the snares. One had closed tight and

had tiny fragments of tortoiseshell-cat fur in it. Two or three had been pushed out of the way, and one had a badger in it – a dead badger which had in its final death throes clawed the bark of the near-by apple tree cordons and cut deep grooves in the ground as it spun itself into a state of strangulation. It's a hell of a death, believe me. A chap in Cambridge wrote a research paper on the snare, and came up with the conclusion that only two animals, the hare and the rabbit, can be humanely snared. The rest of British mammalia aren't structurally suited to a rapid death in a snare, and so strangle to death slowly and very very painfully. Cats and foxes die reasonably quickly as panic causes them to go into paroxysms of frenzy, but a badger, the most phlegmatic of stoats, dies slowly and in great agony. Needless to say, Mr Stone, who is a badger conservationist, was not pleased with Mick and Roger's handiwork. To make matters worse, the night of the snaring saw three of his hens taken.

'We're going to lose permission in those woods,' moaned Mick, 'particularly if one of his cats gets caught up in those snares.'

'Seems likely,' I agreed, both to the losing of the woods and the cat in the snare, for cats seem to go out of their ways to get caught up.

'Trouble is,' Roger continued, 'the woods are alive with foxes and there's no way of taking them.'

I groaned inwardly, for seated opposited Mick was John Cope, and the statement 'the woods are alive with foxes' had gone home. Skins were still fetching a good price – £20 wet – but I had just begun reading for another degree, my back ached something terrible and Merle was really in no fit condition to hunt. He had scars, not serious scars, but few dogs come out from a running battle with a fox without at least a few punctures, punctures which may not appear to fester badly, but which still manage to inject some bacillus. His condition was what must be described as lack lustre and not really up to scratch, particularly for the taxing sport of bowling foxes on the beam, and a dog needs to be in top form for regular fox catching.

It looked like being an icy night, for at four o'clock that afternoon I arrived home in drizzling sleet, the sort of sleet that seeps in through waterproof material, the sort that burrows through one's very bones. A high wind built up, driving the sleet against the window panes, stinging hands and face with ferocity when I stepped out into the night. My spirits picked up. John was a fine-weather hunter and I knew he wouldn't face any night as bleak and forbidding as this. At least, I thought I knew, before there came a knock on the door and John's booming voice.

Facing page: Brough's Earths

119

Fox kills near Stone's wall

'Yer ready then,' he said, tapping his hand with a short shillelagh-like club used to dispatch luckless animal victims.

A curious thought passed through my mind. Only two Romany words have entered into the English language. One is 'cosh', like the weapon Cope was wielding at the moment. The other is 'pal', a word hardly applicable to the chap trying to lure me out into the cold sleet of the night to satisfy his own greed.

'Yer ready, then?' he repeated.

'An hour maybe,' I said, glancing at the window and listening to the stinging sleet hammering on the window pane.

'You gonna salt the area tonight?' (He picked up terms if not skills fairly readily.)

'If they are there in the number Mr Stone says, then salting won't be necessary.'

Besides that, there was a turkey farm near the back of the wood and I'd fetched offal from the pile, driving off foxes to get edible entrails and waste for my dogs when things were bad. Chances were that this midden pile rather than the proximity of Stone's poultry farm caused the foxes to be attracted to the area, for foxes will dine on carrion

'Only two Romany words have entered the English language.
One is "cosh" . . .'

rather than chance their hides by raiding a poultry farm, no matter what children's story books may tell us to the contrary.

The weather continued to worsen, and the hiss of sleet on window pane drowned the hum of my battery charging up near the window. Ten o'clock, eleven o'clock, and not only did the weather continue to be bad, but John looked like staying put in spite of the kind of inclement night that usually deterred, him. He sat there in his Barbour jacket, under which were numerous sweaters, looking like a rotund teddybear or an up-to-date country member of the Pickwick Club, but he was resolute about going out. At 11.20 I resigned myself to the outcome, unplugged my battery, checked its contents and went out to the kennels to fetch Merle.

He was not jumping against his kennel door with his usual enthusiasm, the enthusiasm he usually showed whenever I produced the lamp, but seemed merely resigned to the fact that he, too, was going out on that ghastly night. Secretly I cursed myself for my weak personality, a personality that allowed mental bullies like Cope to badger me into doing things I didn't want to do. I longed for the courage to be able to go in and say, 'Sod off, Copey, I've paid my debt to you a dozen times over. Get out and don't come back with your incredible money-making schemes, that involve my sweat, my dogs, my unhappiness and your pecuniary gain.' But I just didn't have the courage or the eloquence, so 11.30 found me, battery on back, soul in the dumps, jaded lurcher on slip and idiot by my side walking along the lane towards the rear of Mr Stone's walled garden.

We settled in against the wall, shielded somewhat from the sleet and rain by the leafless apple trees, ancient varieties now forbidden by Common Market regulations, a relic of an age when I used to be British. I flashed the beam around the patch of rather open woodland to get the lie of the place, and rather unnecessarily flung a few handfuls of very ripe turkey offal in the clearing to attract any foxes *en route* through to feed on the midden pile. Twelve o'clock and I settled in for the night's misery.

'Christ, it's cold,' said John, and my spirits rose, for I was still prepared to write off the night as a failure and go home.

Quite suddenly, I felt a tingling sensation pass along Merle's spine and his body stiffen. I flicked on the beam, thinking absurdly and unscientifically about how long the light seemed to take to reach the spot baited by the offal. A young male fox, off balance, looked up from the giblets on which he was feeding, his eyes soup-plate huge in amazement. I slipped Merle and my jaded, tired dog was on him in a trice, even before he had time to turn his eyes from the beam and vanish into the darkness of the birch wood. Merle bowled the fox twice, its body and tail turning like a funny Catherine-wheel or one of those margin drawings from a Konrad Lorenz book, and had pinned him by the time John and I arrived to dispatch it quickly and, I must add in the light of recent publicity, painlessly. We retreated back to our post near the wall, the freezing air thick with musk, Merle shaking his head slightly as though to throw off the sting from the bite he must have taken in the face. But we had scarcely time to settle in before I felt Merle stiffen again, and once more prepared to slip him.

Nothing attracts foxes like the scent of foxes, be it the musk left on thistle stalks by a passing male *en route* to seek females or the ripe pungent scent expelled by a fox doing battle with an adversary. I flicked on the beam and found another young male sniffing the cadaver of his fallen brother, for brother it most certainly was, Broughs Earths having had a litter reared in total peace that year. Merle closed with it, cutting it off before it could reach the sanctuary of the rhododendron bushes, and endeavoured to pin it, dodging that snapping, spitting cat-like bite, illuminated in the lamp light. He pinned it with a throat hold while John and I raced up to finish the battle, and in no time flat we were back at the wall, wet, cold yet perspiring freely, waiting for the next fox to pass towards the midden pile.

Merle was panting madly, his breath coming in a deep painful hiss, and it was an hour before he was ready to go again. I think it was Haan who defined fitness as being measured by the length of time a man or beast took to recover from an activity. Merle, like me, was decidedly unfit, and the night's work was playing havoc with him. Twice more I flicked on the beam and twice I found foxes feeding in the clearing or sniffing curiously at the fallen males, but in spite of Cope's urging, Merle was in no condition to go.

An hour or so passed, and three o'clock saw no abatement in the stinging rain, save for the fact that the temperature dropped still further and the rain droplets turned to globules of ice, ice that hung like icicles from the ragged fur around Merle's belly and caused my sodden trousers to crackle when I moved.

Just after three o'clock he ran, bowled and pinned an ancient grey old vixen, with scarred muzzle, whose brown worn and broken teeth bore mute testimony to her antiquity. She must have been the grandmother of half the foxes in the district, and may even have been one of the cubs I brought out of Merioneth twelve years before when distemper, or maybe it was parvo virus, had practically wiped out all the foxes in the district. I regretted killing her, for I had seen her several times during my early morning hunts around the block, but a fox is a fox in the circle of light created by the beam and a worthless skin is indistinguishable from a prime during a rapid jaw-to-jaw catch-as-catch-can battle 'twixt dog and fox. I flashed on the beam to look at her carcass. The skin was moth-eaten, scarred, mangy and probably worth £2, but the writhed lips, the rictus, the result of a sudden and violent death, give the old devil a rather sad look, an appearance that made me think of a once lovely but now geriatric women or Rodin's statue of 'Villon's The Once Beautiful Heaulmière'.

'Skin's worth bugger all,' sniffed John soullessly, and from that moment, by some curious irony, John ceased to be my fellow hunter and became an iconoclast wrapped up in the theology of raking in a fast buck, hell bent on despoiling my countryside, an intruder in my world. We sat near the wall again, Merle unbitten by the last battle and scarcely winded.

Just before four o'clock, I guess, though time began to pass slowly after this hunt, Merle bowled and held another old vixen that had a V-shape cut in her ear, a mark of some encounter, perhaps, or a distinguishing nick put in by some hunter or naturalist to test a theory concerned with foxes. Once she had perhaps been a creature used in a scientific inquiry, now she was simply a cadaver left in a clearing to tempt in other foxes to try their luck.

I had scarcely time mentally to write an elegy over the fallen matron when I sensed yet another fox in the clearing. I say sensed, for I could feel no movement from Merle, no stiffening of his body. Perhaps one's aural acuity becomes more acute as the night wears on, or perhaps one become even more in tune with the dog as a hunt ceases to become exciting and becomes simply an exhausting and jading exercise. I feel it must have been the latter, for as I slipped Merle I sensed his exhaustion almost seeping up the binder twine I used as a slip. He closed with the fox, cutting off its retreat from the bushes, bowling it half-heartedly, losing it, catching it again, pinning it with a none too accurate hold, a hold he released far too soon as soon as I grabbed it. To apportion blame or fault to the next few minutes would be stupid. Merle was in a state of weariness near to exhaustion, and I was in a state of melancholy near to abject misery. So I'll blame Cope. As I grabbed at the fox, it turned, stuck and embedded its fangs in my arm, deep in my arm, and locked like a bulldog. Cope swung his bludgeon madly and I heard Merle squeal and stagger back. The second blow caught my forearm, numbing it, causing massive bruising it later transpired, and the third or fourth blow killed the fox, which slowly, like an action-replay sequence, released its hold on my arm.

I sat down in agony, nursing my twice injured arm, while Merle skulked warily out of range of the madman who had lunged at him. I was too hurt and pained to treat Cope to my usual vehement mouthfuls of dirt.

'You bloody, bloody idiot,' was all I could manage.

'Try for just one more before dawn,' his voice came out of the darkness.

My reply was unrepeatable, and in silence we walked back to the cottage, Cope, thankfully not me, staggering under the weight of seventy pounds of foxes. I examined my arm in the bathroom. It looked a hell of a mess and the prospect of 3B and a tiring day of teaching didn't appeal much. Cope followed me in. He had become Cope now, not John, during our conversations.

'Christ, I'm knackered,' he said, leaning on the sink, gazing in the bathroom mirror, checking on his best side no doubt. 'Going to go to bed,' he yawned. 'Skin us the foxes, Bri,' he threw at me. 'I'm buggered.'

It was to be his last hunt with me, I vowed.

I skinned the foxes before school, my fingers trembling with anger towards Cope and my mind clouded with grizzly thoughts of skinning him. I left the masks on the foxes to allow Mick to show Mr Stone, and was unruffled by Cope's comment, 'You've ruined them skins. They're worth five quid less without the heads still on the skins.'

Mick took all five to Stone's smallholding and basked in the admiration of Mr Stone (taking full credit for the mayhem) while our local postman, not a very good countryman, shook his head in wonder and said, 'You know, I thought they were extinct in Britain.' Perhaps he thought the fourteen-pound carcasses were wolves.

I run ahead of my tale now, and deliberately so for once. Last year Mr Stone dropped off his usual bag of goodies and said, 'You know, Brian, I'm having trouble with foxes again.'

'I'll come up and do them for you,' I yawned, stretching, for Mr Stone has an odd habit of arriving very early in the morning. He gave me a long pitying look.

'No offence, Bri, but could you send up the little fat boy [Mick]. I'd like the job done properly!'

15 *Alec Dowton*

My arm festered in spite of the fact that I cleaned it as best I could
with hot salty water and later with Dettol. A dull throbbing ache
seemed to tingle between my finger tips and my jaw, an ache that my
insane hypochondria instantly labelled angina. A child in my class had
but to touch my arm to have me screaming in agony, and much
against my will I was taken to casualty by one of my friends. ('Should
have stabbed the wound with a red-hot knife and held it until it had
burned out the poison,' put in Moses macabrely. 'The pain would
have probably killed you,' he added wistfully. 'If you die,' he put in,
'can I have your book on game cocks?' I would have thrown
something at him, but my arm was too sore to move.)

At casualty I suffered the indignity of an embarrassing antibiotic
injection.

'Can't I have it in my arm?' I asked timidly.

'Come along,' boomed the voice of a moustached female nurse.
'I've seen hundreds of men's backsides in my time.'

I was about to tell her I didn't want to know about her private life
when the sight of that enormous hypodermic syringe made me hold
my tongue and take my punishment, so to speak. She pumped in a
colossal amount of antibiotic, snorted and left the room, her moustache
twitching with glee.

It did little good – the antibiotic I mean. My arm continued to
throb and the place where the needle went in didn't feel so good
either. What was more alarming still was that angry red lines began
to run up my arm, each one starting from the now badly suppurating
bite. Things didn't look good at all, and even Moses stopped cracking
jokes about amputation. Suddenly it seemed an extremely likely
possibility. That morning I failed to get my swollen arm into my
sleeve and I went to work, coat over shoulders, looking like a rather
effete Shakespearean actor. Every few hours I would unpick the
bandages to survey the damage. It was unpleasant, to say the least,
and now not only ached like hell but also stank. I'd seen such wounds
on dogs: dogs that swelled up like balloons and died. Foxes are foul
feeders, and in spite of their cuddly canine looks are havens for

parasites and bacteria. Their bites invariably fester, and this fox had fed for five days on filth that even Fathom wouldn't eat, so God knew what bugs had been driven into my arms by those carnasial teeth. Merle had recovered from his mauling, but I was in a very bad state of decline.

I think I had reconciled myself to losing at least an arm, and was even prepared for Mo's jokes about one-arm bandits when Alec Dowton called. Now, Alec is an anachronism, a relic of a past age. He is, in fact, a travelling herbalist. The travelling herbalist was a fairly common sight during the Middle Ages, as was the mobile charlatan peddling cure-alls and plant medicines. But in spite of the scorn of historians, many of the remedies sold by these people worked. For instance, Dowton's father, who found a regular customer in my hypochondriac mother, once told her, 'twixt sips of elderberry tea (my mother's staple diet), that if one kept onions hanging in the house then heart disease wouldn't trouble the occupants. With schoolboy intelligence, I ridiculed the statement, but a few years ago a trained doctor wrote a paper literally prescribing raw onions as a diet for thrombosis, for they broke down cholesterol in the blood, and cholesterol is considered by many to be the principal cause of heart disease. Perhaps when modern science and scepticism swept the knowledge of the herbalist under the table, quite a lot was lost. Certainly the Dowtons knew their onions (forgive the pun), and here's a story to illustrate my point.

In 1921, a whooping-cough epidemic swept the valleys of the South Welsh coalfield. Today, with modern medical knowledge and the availability of vaccines, whooping cough may not appear as a serious illness, but in 1921 it saw off a whole load of babies who wheezed, vomitted and gulped themselves into emaciated wrecks before expiring, and dozens of tiny graves in our village churchyard bear mute testimony to the severity of the disease. My sister Margaret, who was four at the time – she is twenty years older than me – went down with the infection. Now, until antibiotics were discovered, medical science had not advanced much since the Middle Ages, so all the doctor advised Mam was to await the outcome of the disease, and judging by the village death rate, the outcome was fairly predictable. Mam gave the situation a great deal of thought and promptly took to her bed – the answer to all Mam's problems; but later that week John Dowton called with his seasonal boxes of elderberry tea, a suitable bribe to lure Mam from her death-bed. By this time my sister was on her way out and the doctor came out with the usual movie doctor cliché, 'It is only a matter of time.' Dowton took one look at my sister, diagnosed the illness instantly (which wasn't difficult, whooping cough being

'. . . if one kept onions hanging in the house, then heart disease
would not trouble the occupant'

fairly obvious) and wrote out a prescription for an infusion on a thin scrap of brown paper that Mam kept to her death.

2 parts ipecac
1 part yarrow
1 part monkshood
1 part mandrake

Mam took the prescription to the local herablist, who blanched at the sight of the ingredients, told her the mix was a formula for a hell brew, but made up the mixture anyway. Margaret was given the infusion, had one of the worst coughing bouts ever, vomitted fit to kill and promptly recovered. End of story about whooping cough, but one more super tale before I go on with my own story, for I find the Dowtons fascinating.

Dowton's father visited the Forest of Dean between the wars, and came in for some stick from the local doctors, who didn't want a charlatan in the village 'spreading nonsense like a medieval witch', and a few sought legal injunctions to stop old man Dowton selling his nostrums. In a near-by village was a case of a seven-year-old girl with an infected ear, an ear suppurating with pus and causing the kid such agony that she raced from room to room screaming and shaking her head to drive away the pain. She was treated by two doctors who did what they could and then gave up as there was little more they could do except wait for the infection to spread to the brain, whereupon death or at least paralysis would follow. As a last resort, the frantic parents – schoolteachers, so Alec believes – called in Alec's father, but the mother 'threw up' when she saw the treatment old man Dowton prescribed. He poulticed the ear with bluebottle maggots and allowed the vile things to eat their fill. Of course, the visiting doctors refused to come near until the 'witch doctor' was thrown off the case, but the child's father allowed the treatment and in a week the girl was cured.

I remember old man Dowton vaguely, but what I do remember clearly was the box of pond water he carried round with him, in which were floating or swimming the vile, obscene-looking horse leeches he used to press against an infected wound so that the leeches could grip with their razor-edged mouths and suck out the venom. Come to think of it, I scoured the local ponds for those leeches, for old man Dowton paid, I think, 6d. (2½p) each for the horrors and I'd have sold my soul for a tanner in those days.

Alec found my arm fascinating and prodded about in the suppurating mess for a few moments. He then went to his van, a vintage Morris 1000, and produced a paper sachet.

'Let's have your arm,' he muttered – an unfortunate choice of phrase, considering the state of the infection – and tipped a yellow powder into the wound. It was obviously simply sulphur, and that couldn't do any harm, so I let him indulge his attempt at quackery. He flung down the empty bag in the hearth and left. My arm felt very hot, and for the first time in my life I had suspicions as to the villainy of the family, so I took the bag plus the remaining yellow powder to Tony Roberts, an analyst friend, and asked him to try his luck at spot-testing the remains in the packet.

'Sulphur,' he said sniffing the bag. 'Harmless enough, but I'll give it a breakdown just to put your mind at ease.'

Two hours later my arm was throbbing like mad and I could scarcely think with the pain. The phone rang.

'Where in hell did you get this mess, Bri?' Tony asked rather anxiously.

I told him.

'It's mostly sulphur,' he explained, 'but for God's sake don't get it on your skin. It's peppered with caustic plant alkaloids like those found in fungi. It can be absorbed through the skin and it can be dangerous,' he threw in as an afterthought.

By this time my arm had been poulticed with the stuff for six hours. I shook my head almost sadly at my own credulity in believing an itinerant who could scarcely write his name. A wave of panic swamped me, but by this time I was too damned tired and ill to do much about it and eager to be to bed. The pain continued to increase.

I must have dozed off at about two o'clock and drifted into a fitful sleep punctuated with horrendous dreams. There were police at my house, dozens of faceless bobbies ransacking the place for nothing in particular, while in the broom cupboard was hanging the neatly butchered remains of Caroline, my boring ex-girlfriend, stupid and predictable as a slice of Battenburg cake. A police officer pushed the butchered cadaver aside and rummaged in the dusters behind it. Clearly he found her just as boring and uninteresting as I did, but at 4.30 I awoke with a blinding headache and the most painful bout of vomiting I have ever experienced. I padded around the bed, feeling for support in the darkness. It was horrendous. Twice I tried to rise and twice I fell back on to the bed too weak to move. I can remember hissing, 'Dowton, you bastard, you've done for me,' like a character out of a Victorian melodrama, but fell back again into a deep sleep, for never have I felt so weak.

At twelve o'clock, noon not midnight, my milkman David began hammering on my front door for payment, and I slithered out of bed and tried to rise. The effort beat me twice, but on the third attempt I staggered to the door, only to hear the milk van – called 'the slowly van' locally – departing. I crawled back indoors and prepared to go back to bed. The sight that greeted me was revolting. My bed was saturated with filth, vomit and urine and the room stank to high heaven. My pillows were soaked with sweat and the stench emerging from the room caused me to throw up again.

I half-staggered, or rather crawled, to the bathroom and turned on the taps to run a bath. As I stretched out my arm I noticed the bandage was slipping off. It was soaked in all manner of vile-smelling filth and blood, but the reason it was slipping off was that the swelling had gone, and though the wound was bleeding badly, the blood was healthy and not poisoned.

'It's probably the antibiotic working,' a doctor friend said, brushing the Dowtons' witchcraft cure aside, but the antibiotic shot was fourteen days old by then, so I was not convinced. Somehow or the other Dowton had come up with some plant recipe – God knows where he discovered it – that not only had an antiseptic quality, but caused poison wounds to gape open and reject their necrotic contents.

'Dowton, you never cease to amaze me,' I said to myself.

Moses was less enthusiastic when I told him the tale.

'*Didikai* can still remember some of the Romany remedies, I suppose,' he conceded. 'Even a *didikai* must know something,' he added disparagingly. 'Personally, I think he's a fake,' he threw in contemptuously, unwilling to give praise to a *didikai*, a traveller without true Romany blood. 'He made a woman some pile suppositories once, and they didn't work at all and they had a horrible taste of liquorice,' he flung in as a rider.

I stopped writing up my diary abruptly and gazed in amazement, shaking my head in wonder, but Mo wasn't listening. He was thumbing through the *Shooting Times* 'Gamekeeper Wanted' advertisements again.

6 *The Final Confrontation*

It had to come, I suppose, partly because keeping the number of dogs which I do confrontations are inevitable, and partly because Vampire is such a fiend that he deliberately provoked supremacy battles just to satisfy his own ego – though whether ego is the correct word to apply to a dog may be a bit questionable. As he aged, he grew more rather than less fractious and more intolerant to the idiosyncrasies of puppies. He now walked about the run with his lips permanently bared as if defying the world to approach him. Just occasionally he would thrash an erring or boisterous puppy to keep his hand in, so to

The night of the final battle with Vampire

speak, but the grown dogs simply kept out of his way when he stalked the run. Fractious, irritable, vicious, he was sliding into senility a mass of scars, resentment and hostility, a biological timebomb ready and willing to explode for the slightest reason. In spite of his uses, he was not a dog I could honestly say that I liked, nor was he a type of dog I would willingly breed again.

I had kept Merle out of his way since that awful skirmish, the battle that all but crippled and damn-nigh killed Merle, partly because exercising lurchers and terriers in the same compound may suit some, but I find it a source of worry. A terrier gets brushed or stepped on by a lurcher and the terrier snaps at the lurcher, as most terriers are prone to do. The lurcher retaliates and all hell is let loose, which usually results in a crippled lurcher or a dead terrier. Likewise, I find anyone who keeps a lurcher and terrier together using a terrier to flush quarry and a lurcher to catch is well on the way to having what I call a broken team. Let me explain: terrier (a very possessive type of animal) flushes rabbit. Lurcher catches same and tries to retrieve to hand. Terrier runs up and hangs on rabbit, claiming it as his own. Lurcher retaliates and there is havoc or, worse still, a lurcher that refuses to retrieve to hand and runs off with the rabbit. Hence I try to keep my terriers and lurchers separate, but it isn't always easy.

It had already been a devilish week for fights. Omega had bickered with Beltane, her great-great-aunt, non-stop for several days, and Pagan had aided and abetted the pair, just begging for something to start. The air in the run was thick with resentment and the atmosphere electric. When one keeps a pack of terriers and lives with them, I suppose one becomes part of the pack, albeit an auxiliary *persona non grata* member, and it is easy to sense the build up to 'a real bad one'. Every death struggle in the run, and I have had a few, had been expected and predicted. One learns to think and move with terrier speed to prevent really bad fights taking place. Dealers, men who buy and sell dogs – making a business of canine misery, I call it – can never become really *sympatico* with the feelings of a terrier pack, for the pack is not a series of individuals, it is a unity and usually functions as one. When there are bad hunts, all the hunters hunt badly. When there is an air of aggression, all, even the epsilon category terriers, the cringers, the fawners, the sycophants, are aggressive. Individuality of spirit is not to be encouraged in a terrier pack if the pack is to function properly.

The warning light flashed on momentarily on the Thursday night during the hunt when Alan Thomas came up from South Wales, bringing his two Lakeland terriers. We arrived at the venue about ten minutes before Alan, and my trailer had already disgorged its dogs before Alan's car arrived, Vampire spending the intervening minutes strutting about the yard stiff-legged, snarling at nothing in particular and everything in general. The other dogs quite simply kept out of his way, deliberately moving out of his path as he came roaring and snarling towards them like a public-school bully. Such menacing usually precedes each and every hunt, but as soon as the action begins, the tension is gone, the pack suddenly swings into being and every dog works as one of a team. But minutes preceeding the start of a hunt are often a bit hair-raising.

Alan arrived, turned loose the two Lakelands, and havoc erupted. Vampire must have been sniffing at the car doors, so was aware of their presence, but before they had hit the floor he had torn into them, bowling both by the sheer fury of his rush and seizing Chanter, the bigger of the two, by the throat. The first holds, the first bites of a fight, are really catch holds and are rarely serious grips for a dog with fighting bull-terrier blood usually shifts his grip two or three times before he adheres with his final murderous catch hold. Vampire, however, connected first time with a bite straight across the throat of the dog, a bite that would crush the epiglottis and throttle the air out of his unwilling combatant. It was a straightforward bite, put in quickly and accurately, but it required Alan's fifteen stone standing on a bar across Vampire's throat to make Vampire release his hold. It was a nasty, unpleasant incident, but by Saturday Vampire was well and truly worked up for the big battle and it needed very little heat to trigger off the fuse.

It would be right, I suppose, to keep to my image as a stock keeper to say that Roger's negligence caused the fight that came that Saturday afternoon, but it wouldn't be accurate and it would be a bit unfair. Vampire was spoiling for a fight, strolling around stiff-legged, lips raised as if defying anything to come near. Two or three times he thrashed offending puppies, bowling Rollo, his fat, inoffensive great-grandson, pinning him by the face and shaking the screaming babe half to death.

I sent Roger to fetch the handbroom from the whelping sheds while I put Vampire away, for his evil temper and foul tantrums were causing me considerable annoyance. As I glanced up I saw Merle following Roger into the run. Vampire must have seen him at the same moment, for he let out a lion-like roar and hurled himself forward. It seems unlikely that he could have remembered the trouncing he once gave the infant Merle and decided to finish the job. What is more likely is that, in his current mood, any dog, particularly any large dog, would have produced the same reaction. One moment Vampire was standing by my feet, the next he was launching himself through the air at Merle, hell bent on mangling, maiming, killing this inane-looking beast who had had the temerity to venture into his domain.

I had expected Merle, who is a sensible, quiet, unobtrusive dog, to run, to high-tail it away from the battle, or quite simply to roll on his back in a submissive gesture, a gesture Vampire would find it irresistible not to follow up, I'm afraid. As it happened, Merle did neither. He simply stood there like a fool, waiting for Vampire's rush. I shouted to Roger to stop the head-on collision, for I had visions of Merle mauled, with a shoulder ripped out or at least rendered *hors de combat* for a week or so, but Roger had seen the result of getting between Vampire and a victim and seemed less than enthusiastic about stepping between the pair. Merle, however, seemed totally unruffled by the forthcoming collision. Vampire leaped the last two feet, straight into Merle's face, his lips writhed and teeth bared.

At the moment of impact, as I was calculating the vet's fees, Merle turned and snatched, seizing Vampire as he had seized his first fox, flinging him as a terrier would seize a rat, hurling him across the run. Before Vampire could recover from the shock of impact, Merle was on him, pinning him with the usual fox-fixing throat hold, a bite totally covering the wind-pipe, giving the throat a slight shake for better purchase, but throttling the life out of Vampire. I raced in to stop the carnage, and Merle, thinking I had secured Vampire as I secured each and every fox he pinned, released his hold. It was a mistake. Vampire rolled clear and resumed his attack, screaming like a banshee in frustrated rage at this dog who had had the gall to face him. But again at the moment of impact Merle side-stepped him, flung him and pinned him, holding him effortlessly in his jaws as if the whole process was child's play. In the run, agitated by the skirmishing, Beltane had set about Omega and Pagan had pitched into attack both or whoever looked like losing, for such is Pagan's way. My concern was with the death-struggle taking place near the kennels.

Again I approached and again Merle, thinking I had Vampire secure, slipped his hold and released Vampire, who again flew at him with fury. I turned to stop the skirmish that was now involving Pagan, Battle, Beltane, Omega and Witch, clubbing, kicking, throwing dogs over the fence into Barlow's field, receiving several savage bites as I did so. It took maybe two minutes to stop the mauling, two minutes that resulted in a badly bitten Witch and an ear torn from Battle, and when I returned to the main fight, Merle had all but strangled Vampire. I closed with them and Merle again released his hold and Vampire staggered to his feet, fell, rose again and fell. With

Beltane

a gargantuan effort, he tottered upright, and with a roar that failed to emerge from his torn throat, he again tried to attack. Merle struck, flung him and stood back unmarked and unmoved by the battle, his gay tail held at a jaunty angle, awaiting the next attack, while I kennelled up the sobbing, panting terrier. Three days later, while I was ratting Vampire, I noticed he was failing to kill with his usual dexterity. I examined him. His jaws had been smashed like matchwood.

We talked of the fight with Moses that night, marvelling at Merle's skill in overcoming the old warrior.

Mo spat in disgust. 'Jesus, he weighs over sixty pounds and the old bugger just twelve. What hope did he have against a lurcher?'

I didn't answer. Strange, that: I had never considered Vampire to be a 'small dog'.

Epilogue

That ghastly winter came to an end and I took stock of my situation. True, I'd made a few firm fox-eating friends at the local Chinese restaurant, but I was financially less well off than I'd ever been. Cope had gone, never to return, driven away by my indifference to him after our hunt at Stones Wall, so I suppose I should be thankful for small mercies. He'd made over £1,000 cash selling skins from foxes caught by my ugly, but useful dog, however, and had pocketed the lot without so much as a thank you.

At the end of the winter, a few days before spring officially arrived, I bought a tin of corned beef from a musty little corner shop, a few miles from my cottage, one of those corner shops described so well by Benny Green, shops rich in character, but richer still in bacteria. Next day I went down with a terrible case of food poisoning that racked my body with pain and damned nigh killed me. Ian Bullock, one of my fourth-form boys, phoned me repeatedly that day, and when the phone wasn't answered sensed something was wrong and walked the thirteen miles from Walsall, arriving at the cottage in the nick of time, I think, for another icy night in an unheated house would have just about seen me off. He cleaned up my house, propped me up and then quite suddenly he said, 'You're too old for this sort of life, sir. Give it up.'

A year previous I would have been angry at his impudence. Now, propped up with cushions and pillows, feeling as weak as water, I realized he was correct. Ten years before I should have treated the icy winter as a joke, a test of my manhood, perhaps. Now I was weakened by its havoc and no longer capable of taking the freezing nights out hunting, nights I once used to enjoy.

I lay up for a week as a result of the food poisoning, knowing my dogs and ferrets were being cared for by Ian and one of his classmates, but after five days of bed I tottered down the run to see Merle. He looked ghastly, his fur staring, his ribs showing and wounds that could have given an RSPCA official every reason to issue a summons against me. Most of his ribs had been fractured by flying tackles at foxes, and stroking his chest felt like touching a rosary, each lump representing a bad rib injury. His face had a lop-sided look, the result of four really bad jaw-to-jaw catch holds and his appearance was positively hideous.

'You should be shot for keeping a bloody dog like this,' Mo shouted, and for once I knew he was right. I gave Merle a quick examination, put him under a heat lamp to assist his recovery and decided to retire him.

I glanced back at the dog lying in the straw illuminated by the heat lamp's rays. Hell, he was ugly, and I'd have been a very wise man to be able to predict that he would become the start of a dynasty, but that, as they say in the very best of fairy tales, is another story.